Philosophy from a Skeptical Perspective

One of the questions that philosophers discuss is, How can we
avoid – or, at least, reduce – errors when explaining the world?
The skeptical answer to this question is that we cannot avoid errors
because no statement is certain or even definitely plausible, but we
can eliminate some past errors. Philosophers invest much effort in
attempts to refute skepticism because it strikes them as contrary to
common sense, but they have met with no shred of success. The
reason is simple: common sense actually sides with skepticism rather
than against it. But, philosophers see things differently because they
derive from skepticism unreasonable corollaries. These corollaries
are indeed unreasonable, yet their derivations are all invalid. To
illustrate the reasonableness of our version of skepticism, we draw
attention repeatedly to diverse practical consequences of our discussions. These consequences bring philosophy down to Earth and
comprise an outline of a skeptical guide to the real world, no less;
however, like all guides, it is imperfect. This book advocates the skeptical position and discusses its practical applications in science, ethics,
aesthetics, and politics.

Joseph Agassi is professor emeritus at Tel Aviv University and York
University, Toronto. He is the author of more than four hundred
contributions, including more than twenty books, on a variety of
topics in philosophy.

Abraham Meidan is an independent scholar of philosophy. He is
Chief Executive Officer of WizSoft, a data-mining software company;
Chairman of the Board of Afeka Engineering College in Tel Aviv; and
Chairman of Targetech Innovation Center.

Philosophy from a Skeptical Perspective

JOSEPH AGASSI

Tel Aviv University

ABRAHAM MEIDAN

Independent Scholar

CAMBRIDGE
UNIVERSITY PRESS

CAMBRIDGE UNIVERSITY PRESS
Cambridge, New York, Melbourne, Madrid, Cape Town, Singapore, São Paulo, Delhi

Cambridge University Press
32 Avenue of the Americas, New York, NY 10013-2473, USA

www.cambridge.org
Information on this title: www.cambridge.org/9780521726399

First published 2008

Printed in the United States of America

A catalog record for this publication is available from the British Library.

Library of Congress Cataloging in Publication Data

Agassi, Joseph.
Philosophy from a skeptical perspective / Joseph Agassi, Abraham Meidan.
    p.   cm.
Includes bibliographical references (p.   ) and index.
ISBN 978-0-521-89812-6 (hardback) – ISBN 978-0-521-72639-9 (pbk.)
1. Skepticism.   I. Meidan, Abraham, 1949–   II. Title.
B837.A33   2008
149′.73 – dc22   2007048051

ISBN   978-0-521-89812-6 hardback
ISBN   978-0-521-72639-9 paperback

Contents

Preface

For more than two centuries, the mainstream rationalist tradition in philosophy took it for granted that its chief role was to respond to the skeptic challenge. It is not quite clear why, for the challenge rests on the assumption that there is nothing to skepticism, that it is not serious, that it is obviously answerable. If so, why bother with it? Moreover, if it is so obviously faulty, why is it so hard to answer? Why do so many philosophers see it as so terrible and threatening to our sanity?

Skepticism is dangerous, most philosophers explain, because it is paralyzing. It is easy to show that this observation is obviously false; skeptics suffer from paralysis no more than other people. Remarkably, critics of skepticism use this observation as an even stronger argument against skepticism. People who claim that they are skeptics are not paralyzed; hence, it follows logically that they only pretend to be skeptics. Yet their preaching, the critics of skepticism continue, however flippant it is, can nonetheless cause harm by spreading discouragement. It is obvious they conclude their argument, that doubt discourages.

All this is very convincing; we do not know why. For, obviously, it is far from the truth: skeptics are not paralyzed because skepticism does not always paralyze. In truth, every philosophy moves some people to action and others to inaction. Indeed, in a crisis, under conditions of utter ignorance, often some spirited people take the lead, do something, and become leaders just because of the sane conviction that any action is better than inaction. Skeptics take this to be common, whereas their critics assume that conduct follows according to assured tradition or scientific ideas, to those that underwent the process of strict verification. But, actually, there is no such assurance. In addition, motivation – however following whatever chain of causality – is still quite distinct from logical conclusions following invariably from any premise. Why then do we prefer some conduct to others? Can a skeptic explain this as reasonable? The answer is: only up to a point.

With patience and diligence, let us strive to pinpoint the difficulties that mainstream and skeptic philosophers meet facing each other. On the whole, we are willing to enter any subfield of philosophy where the dispute rages. But, we limit our discussion to the reasonable or rationalist arguments. We have little interest in discussing the arguments that seem to us not worthy of critical response.

Here, we survey the reasonable literature devoted to skepticism, where we take even the slightest degree of reasonableness as sufficient for comment, brief or detailed, as the situation warrants. We do so with a slant toward the practical applications because their reasonableness is easier to spot and easier to agree with and because it is a common error that skepticism is impractical. Also, we contribute to the correction of two great, widespread, expensive mistaken views: that philosophy is barren and that all disputes (especially philosophical) are practically harmful. Engaging in philosophical disputes about any activity can improve that activity, we claim, even if the dispute about it will never be settled. For any dispute may eliminate some perceived errors and thereby help remove waste of efforts in wrong directions. And, arguing that people waste their lives on worthless activities may help prevent wasting lives on worthless ends even though we will never know for sure what ends are worthy.

In our presentation, we follow the traditional rules of discourse, the ones that Bernard Russell and Karl Popper have stressed and followed:

1. In philosophical (as any other) activity, one should say why it matters. This runs contrary to Ludwig Wittgenstein's assertion that philosophy is inherently "idle"; that the sole task of honest philosophy is to resolve confusion.
2. Philosophical (as any other) texts can and should be as clear and understandable as possible, hopefully well enough to be open to criticism. This runs contrary to the opaque style of many philosophers, particularly the existentialists among them and particularly if it is a means for escaping possible criticism.

In line with these precepts, this book addresses all curious readers; basic training in philosophy suffices.

We advocate skepticism quite openly. We consider no statement certain, demonstrable, plausible, or otherwise justified in the epistemological sense of these terms. We present repeatedly alternative versions of reasonability that, we contend, are both skeptical and commonsensical. We apply this thesis to epistemology, ethics, politics, and aesthetics.

We reject offhand the relativist position that all theories are equally serious (or equally unserious) so that anything goes, for we deny that skepticism implies relativism in any way. Clearly, by its own light, relativism is not serious. Nevertheless, some philosophers take it seriously and with great regret – only because they erroneously consider relativism a corollary to skepticism. Others try hard to refute skepticism and they are very sad to admit that they have failed; however, they remain convinced that skepticism is false simply because relativism is. Yet the truth remains: skepticism is true and relativism is false.

There are three ideas that people often consider together: skepticism, the idea that no position is demonstrable; relativism, the idea that there is no absolute truth; and nihilism, the idea that all ideas are of equal value. Admittedly, relativism implies nihilism. Nevertheless, we know of thinkers who advocated any one of these three ideas and any two of them. What is important for us here is that skepticism need not be nihilist. This is so just because not all versions of skepticism are relativist. Similarly, not all versions of relativism are skeptical; Wittgenstein, it seems, was a relativist but not a skeptic.[1] Most of his works are devoted to combat skepticism and, perhaps to that end, he – at times, at least – felt the need to endorse relativism. Whether this is so is under dispute among Wittgenstein's disciples, and it is not for us to adjudicate. Rather, our starting point is the advocacy of skepticism and the rejection of relativism and more so of nihilism.

Indeed, we consider relativism and nihilism versions of irrationalism: their advocates oppose rationality or, at least, they judge rationality to be insignificant. But perhaps this is not so; perhaps relativists are not skeptics and they use skepticism only to prove their point, for skepticism is used quite often as a weapon in the hands of people

---

[1] Wittgenstein, in his *Philosophical Investigations* (§109), said, "And we are not permitted to present any kind of theory. Nothing hypothetical is allowed in our considerations." (Authors' translation; but perhaps we misread this: he was a notoriously obscure writer.)

who do not advocate it in the least. This is true of irrationalists in general and of some relativists in particular: they employ skeptical arguments although they do not consider skepticism to be true. Most of them are committed to one dogma or another and are even proud of it, considering open-mindedness frivolous and any expression of skepticism sheer levity, the lack of commitment based on flippancy. Therefore, they limit their use of skepticism to their struggle against reason: if rationalism were true, then its adherents could refute skepticism; but, indeed, they cannot. Nevertheless, everybody can try to be open-minded and invite criticism, and this we heartily recommend.

We try to come as close as possible to relativism without the loss of rationality and without falling into nihilism: we should not forget how very important and responsible it is to use our brains, poor as they admittedly are. We claim that the best way to achieve this is by adopting pluralism but never categorically. Pluralism may raise the ability to behave in a responsible, open-minded way, but only if it does not sanction any silly view, if it is not nihilist. The nihilist sort of open-mindedness that does not oppose any idea, no matter how silly, is flippant indeed. We should not adopt pluralism out of indifference: relativists tend to do so in the hope of avoiding all disagreements; with the intent of avoiding disputes, they make light of all differences between competing ideas. We take pluralism as resting on ignorance: ideas are important, and we disagree because we do not know which of the alternative options is true and because we know that quite possibly we are all in error. The truth is still eluding us, but we do not lose heart. The attitude that we advocate limits pluralism to the exclusion of ideas that are known as effectively criticized, as long as the criticism of them is left unanswered. On this, we have an important disagreement with the relativists. They may feel obliged to admit that despite their relativism, they disallow some utterly unacceptable ideas. Yet, they admit this only under duress and they do not see this as the refutation of their relativism. This leads us to also oppose relativism as one of the objectionable ideas that our moderate pluralism does disallow. Nihilism is another such idea, which is possibly a part of relativism. Thus, we consider our moderate pluralism a sign of poverty: our ignorance is unavoidable but it is still undesirable and we should always fight it as best we can. Therefore, we consider it progress whenever an idea that our moderate pluralism has admitted becomes no longer admissible as a result of some valid criticism; we likewise consider it progress whenever a new idea is conceived and found admissible to moderate pluralism. It is useful to apply this policy to relativism and to as many other ideas as possible while remaining rationalists – namely, while excluding the views that seem to us effectively criticized. Therefore, whenever it is possible and not too cumbersome, we try to rectify a refuted idea so that in its modified version it can remain an open option.

This policy we apply not only to relativism but also to all other ideas that we criticize throughout this book. Consider psychological reductionism, the idea that all thinking can be fully reduced to psychological concepts. We come as close as possible without losing rationality; we do acknowledge that psychology is largely responsible for our sense of what is true, good, and beautiful; but we reject the idea that the meanings of these concepts can be reduced to pure psychology.

Thus, our view is closest to what David Hume wanted his philosophy to be; moderate skepticism, he called it. We achieve his aim with ease because we employ tools that were not available to him. He was unable to free himself from the traditional, classical idea that rationality equals proof. As long as we do not explicitly reject the classical identification of rationality with proof (or with proof-surrogates), the slightest concession to skepticism makes us (unwittingly, perhaps, or even against our expressed wish) vulnerable to the charge of relativism and its allure. Yet, insistence on the idea that proof is possible is dogmatic, especially in the face of Hume's criticism. This intolerable dilemma has hounded philosophy between Hume and Popper. Even Russell admitted in the eve of his life that he was caught in this dilemma, having (rightly) found relativism too tolerant and classical rationalism too rigid. All his life he searched for a middle ground and he finally admitted that he could not find it. It is thus no surprise that Popper's philosophy stands out so. Even Russell could not stomach it because he found it too pessimistic. In this, he was in error: we must judge it pessimistic if we cling to the view that only the demonstrable is valuable. But, if we consider the vast progress that science has achieved without proof, then we may very well opt for optimism.

If one tries to find another philosophy that resembles Popper's to some degree, one has to go as far as the theology of the great medieval thinker, Moses Maimonides, who said it is impossible for mere humans to know what the Lord is, only what He is not, but it behooves us to try repeatedly. Taking seriously the modern move from theology to natural science, his so-called negative theology translates into negative natural philosophy. This takes us even further back, to the Socratic idea that even though we cannot find out what is true, we are able to find out what is false and try to avoid it. This way of thinking annoys some, perhaps because of the fear of becoming irrationalist. It seems to others just right, particularly for science: laws of nature preclude some states of affairs (for example, bodies lighter than water cannot sink by themselves, or, energy of a closed system cannot increase). The state of affairs that does exist is a window of opportunity that at times we make use of but not necessarily with any understanding. Indeed, action usually precedes thinking, at least such actions that are as essential to life as the intake of air and nourishment. Scientific research is the effort to explain these opportunities, and the explanations often point to new opportunities for us to try. But, the whole venture is as much due to our good fortune (usually called the grace of God) as it is to our very presence on this Earth. Some like this because it sounds religious; others hate it for the very same reason. We ourselves are indifferent to such similarities – until and unless we find ourselves too naïve or credulous.

Scientific explanation links events – happy or unhappy as they may be; hence, windows of opportunity – to their ostensible causes. We can imagine which opportunity has led to the cause by assuming another causal explanation. Suppose that we could, in this way, regress in time as far as possible; we still assume some cause that together with the laws of nature links certain current events to other antecedent events. But can we ever similarly hope to explain any and all events? Alas, no, our current theory of explanation does not allow this. To echo Albert Einstein, our model of causal explanation leaves unanswerable the question: Why is there anything in this world of ours?

Again, some like this idea very much because they find in it license for their religious preferences; others hate it for the very same reason. We find both these responses excessive. As Immanuel Kant said, our ignorance is no ground for any specific speculation; at the very best, it is compatible with too many.

Finally, we offer a word about the systematic engagement throughout this book with the psychological aspects of philosophical problems.

Traditional philosophy developed the theories of scientific method and scientific knowledge as a psychology of learning and of knowledge. This begs the question, of course, because psychology should be a science proper, not the foundation of science. The great advance in twentieth-century philosophy was the move from psychology to sociology; from the traditional questions of how do I learn and how do I know to the questions of how do we learn and how do we know. This change opened new vistas touched on often throughout this work. Indeed, the new circumstance begs question no less than the old because we want our sociology to be scientific as well. Hence, such progress makes sense only if philosophy becomes fallibilist; that is, if it admits that we can claim that no theory is error-free. Also, the major defect of the traditional theory – namely, that its psychology is not sophisticated – does have a parallel in the new theory: fortunately, the necessary part of the sociology of the new philosophy is trite and asserts hardly more than that the funds of knowledge are not individual but rather social (institutional). In any case, the change invites a replacement from the old to the new style of both the psychological and sociological aspects of learning. This change in sociology is easy and it has led to the growth of a new scientific field: the sociology of science. This change in psychology is still waiting its turn, although it is clearly both significant and challenging. In this book, we undertake a beginning in this direction, and we differ from tradition at least in our stress on the limitations within which we conceive this project. We suggest that it is at least useful for philosophers who find the transition from the traditional to the new to be a difficult one. And, because they are still in the majority, we hope that this book speaks to them as well.

The first draft of this book was written by Abraham Meidan, and was partly based on his previous book, *Skepticism is True.* Joseph Agassi then broadened and elaborated on it, with the manuscript going back and forth in the usual manner of co-authorship.

Tel Aviv, Fall 2007

Acknowledgments

We are grateful to Dr. Chen Yehezkeli and Professor Ian Jarvie for their comments on the penultimate draft; to Aaron Agassi for his many suggestions for improvements to the presentation; to Maggie Meitzler and her staff for the highly professional copyediting; and to Beatrice Rehl, philosophy editor for Cambridge University Press, and her readers for their encouragement and their penetrating and very helpful critical comments.

1

Introduction

Philosophy consists of attitudes toward life or ways of life and inquiries in such regard, and they come in a great variety, of course. Philosophical tradition displays a regular bias in favor of the life of contemplation and equanimity. There was an effort to displace these values with a new tradition – nineteenth-century Romanticism – that emulated the heroes and despots of old and likewise glorified the life of achievements, especially great ones, military and political. The rise of brutal regimes that pride themselves on such achievements has somewhat attenuated the popularity of this enduring and sadistic tradition but, alas, not to the point of extinction.

Philosophical inquiries traditionally center on a small set of questions that presumably signify the choice of an attitude toward life or a way of life. Socrates, the father of Western philosophy, asserted his philosophy of life in his famous slogan: "the unexamined life is not worth living." His way of life was devoted to preaching this idea by challenging people to examine their own life: he moved throughout the day from one place where people gathered to another, challenging the opinions of anyone who would accept his challenge.

Here are examples of questions that raise discussions that tradition considers philosophical. What are things made of? What kinds of things are there in the world? Is the soul immortal? How can we avoid errors when we seek explanations (of physical or mental events)? What are the right principles of the right moral conduct? What is the best political regime? Such questions sally forth in quest for the very best, even though we know that the very best is unattainable because we are not divine. But the quest for the idea of the best is the quest for criteria; to find what we would deem the best is to find a

criterion for judging some action or thing as the best – or even some
action or thing as better than some other action or thing, which is very
useful.

Like all intellectual activities, philosophy is, in part, the search for
good ideas – that is, for ideas, theories, and general truths that have
intellectual value. Philosophy thus shares this search with religion (or
theology), mathematics, and science in an effort to explain the world
around us and adjust as best as possible. In this respect, philosophical, mathematical, and scientific research are partners in a venture,
moving along in different regions of the territory that they share –
whether in cooperation, in a division of labor, or at times in serious
competition, whatever the case may be. People engaged in any kind
of research show no interest in a detailed catalogue of discrete points
of information that would fill a telephone directory, no matter how
practical and useful. Useful things may be most uninteresting; the
more accurate they are, the more useful, but even the most accurate are at times merely useful. Rather, researchers seek theories –
that is, general statements (statements that begin with the word *all*)
that explain known phenomena and results, however puzzling and
fascinating. These observations are themselves general or particular, and their explanations then belong to the generalizing and the
historical sciences, respectively. Of course, some people invest much
effort in collections of all sorts, from butterflies to stamps. Many people admit that these collections can be fascinating, and researchers
may find them useful, but they are scarcely scientific unless they are
accompanied by theoretical considerations. Thus, the difficult and
interesting question imposes itself on butterfly collectors: What is a
butterfly?

Opinions keep changing. Agendas keep changing, too, but less
rapidly. This is true of both philosophical and scientific inquiries; however, notoriously philosophical agendas are much slower to change.
Some people suggest that they never change, so they refer to the
agenda of philosophy as a hardy perennial. They exaggerate. We can
easily detect change even regarding the philosophical question about
our intellectual agenda: What is it and what should it be? In the Middle
Ages, theology was at the top of the philosophical agenda and then
exited almost entirely in the seventeenth century. To the end of the

eighteenth century, what was then called natural philosophy and what we now consider science (e.g., physics, biology) was considered an integral part of philosophy. Later, some of the research was gradually recognized as independent studies. Physics and chemistry came into their own first; biology and mathematics followed suit. In the twentieth century, science became identical to empirical science,[1] with physics as its paradigm; thus, modernist philosophers expelled mathematics from the field of science (and perhaps kicked upstairs to the field of logic): questions concerning science ceased to affect it. "To the extent that the statements of mathematics represent reality," said Einstein in a memorable dictum, "they are not certain, and to the extent that they are certain, they do not represent reality." These changes were completed by the middle of the nineteenth century. The question was soon raised: Why? And this question still engages many philosophers today, filling the philosophical literature. Medicine gained scientific recognition only in the early twentieth century, impacted more by Louis Pasteur's discovery than anything else. Mental illness entered science through the back door, as medicine. Psychology proper (especially studies of perception, learning, and child development) was left behind and became a major part of the impoverished field of philosophy. Some still view it this way, considering what they call "philosophical psychology" or the "philosophy of the mind" to be a major philosophical preoccupation. Psychology itself already has a part that is generally viewed as scientific, particularly perception theory – or at least some parts of it. The rest of psychology, including psychopathology and learning theory, is still in the process of becoming a science or gaining scientific recognition. Some psychologists claim that in the psychological research they carry out, they follow procedures known as scientific and that this elevates their research to the status of a science; therefore, their field should be recognized as such. Many psychological discussions still appear in the philosophical literature, including the discussion of the question: Does psychology deserve the status of

---

[1] This is not quite accurate: in German-speaking countries, the concept of "dogmatic sciences" is still common; it denotes theology, legal studies, and such. This comes up in many cross-linguistic debates, irritatingly in attempts to clear confusions and confusingly in attempts to gloss over disagreements about what makes science empirical.

a science and, if so, which of its theories belong to science proper and why? Some psychological research is obviously not scientific, or not yet.

In this sense, perhaps philosophy is the research into questions that have not (yet) developed into sciences. And perhaps it is the hothouse of domains of interests and research destined to go out into the world and gain scientific status. This was the idea that the great philosopher Bertrand Russell advocated early in the twentieth century (in his rightly celebrated introductory *The Problems of Philosophy*). He did not say, however, what examination a field or a theory should pass in order to graduate as a science proper, so we do not know if, in his view, philosophy itself might one day pass the same test. He did want this: he said his life ambition was to contribute to the process of philosophy becoming scientific. He pointed out that one condition for a theory to be scientific is accessibility – at the very least, a theory must be on public display and clear before it can be declared scientific. Russell raised the level of clarity of philosophy to such a height that those whom he influenced speak and write much more clearly than was the rule before his time. We hope that, at least in this respect, he has influenced us as well, that he has taught us how to be a little clearer than we would otherwise be. It is not easy to express oneself clearly, least of all in philosophy.

Russell wanted both science and philosophy to be as free as possible of obscure language and mystical ideas. He appreciated every case of a science being liberated from the yoke of philosophy; this is a liberation movement of sorts. Apart from obscure language and mysticism, what is this yoke from which science should free itself? We discuss this question later in this book. For the time being, however, let us make do with the mention of just one important idea about the difference between science and philosophy, one that has gained common recognition. Philosophical discussions may raise doubts about any statement, no matter how obvious it seems. Scientific discussions are more limited: they take much for granted. For example, all discussions about any theory of chemistry leave no room for doubt about the existence of matter or water; one who is doubtful should move to the seminars of the philosophy department. This, to repeat, is common wisdom. Being philosophers, we permit ourselves to doubt that it is true. Is it? If yes, why? If not, why is it so popular despite its being erroneous? We return to these questions in due course as well.

The Practical Side of Philosophy

All this may lead to the conclusion that, unlike science, philosophy is devoted to discussions of questions that have no practical significance, discussions that bear no useful fruit. Not so: although much of the effort to do away with skepticism is useless (as well as uninteresting), many of the interesting questions discussed within philosophy are practical and many of the interesting questions discussed within science are not.

We find nothing dishonorable in discussions that have no practical value, especially when they are interesting and more so when they challenge our prejudices. Moreover, even if one does not value impractical questions, one has to admit that some of the most impractical discussions turned out in time to be of great practical value, so that even the preference for the practical has to make room for the impractical. ("What is the use of a child?" Benjamin Franklin asked rhetorically in this context.) Moreover, we do not quite know what we consider practical; this depends on our values, and the discussion of values traditionally lies at the very heart of philosophy.

For example, the Copernican Revolution was of great practical value because it improved astronomical predictions, which determine future calendars; as long as most people are religious, the calendar is of tremendous practical importance. Indeed, although the Church of Rome officially questioned the theoretical status of Copernicus' theory, it admitted its practical value and even had missionaries teach Chinese astronomers how to use it. The distinction between use and assent was so tremendous that the terminology of the Catholic Church at the time distinguished clearly between practical and philosophical valuation, where the philosophical assent to a theory was the assertion that it is true. Yet, it was the impractical side of Copernican astronomy that mattered, said Galileo, thereby risking his life. It was the root of the scientific revolution that, as it happened, triggered the industrial revolution.

The great philosophical question of the time was: Is it better to follow tradition or to trust one's own judgment? This question is not as easy as it sounds because we know that individual funds of knowledge are much poorer than the traditional knowledge – the latter is the product of efforts made over generations in the society in which the individual lives. No single individual possesses so much knowledge, and even combining all the knowledge of any group of friends or colleagues is no substitute for traditional knowledge. To avail oneself of a significant portion of public knowledge, one has to integrate into society and abide by its rules. We do not know what this amounts to, but clearly it is significant.

Many conservative thinkers find themselves, against their will, leading revolutions of all sorts: intellectual, scientific, moral, and even political. Copernicus and Galileo are examples as are the many people who followed them and agreed that tradition is no substitute for individual freedom of thought, that it is impossible to demand people to follow tradition when they see its defects no matter how valuable it may be. This attitude about tradition, the moderate skepticism about it, is one that is very common in the West, but it received articulation only after World War II. This very articulation is the achievement of recent philosophy – of Karl Popper, to be precise. It is the outcome of a most abstract research project and is of great practical value as individual freedom.

So much for the praise of impractical thinking. Again, we deem impractical thinking essential for cultural existence and, therefore, of the highest practical value for the extra worth that culture brings to our lives. Nevertheless, one way or another, this book centers on philosophical questions known to have valuable practical implications – simply because this is a sadly neglected aspect of philosophy that creates much harmful misconception. Also, we admit that we like to be helpful.

Some of the practical implications of philosophy derive from philosophical theories. An obvious and well-known example is Marxism, which is a philosophical theory that made great change in the world of political and economic practice. Unfortunately, some of these changes were for the worse; fortunately, not all of them were. Nevertheless, this is a different matter: after we agree as to what philosophy is and that it has practical implications, we may continue the discussion and find out under what conditions which practical implications of which theories are good, which are bad. So we should first take note of how Marxism – like many other theories – has practical implications, and then ask which of these are good and which are bad and why. Some may say that this is irrelevant because Marxism is not a philosophy but rather a science. This idea was common among followers of Marx during his lifetime and even later, but it is no longer popular. If one is tempted to cut things short, saying that philosophy has no good practical implications, we can likewise cut short the discussion and mention that some of the greatest and most influential ideas began as philosophical theories, including the ideas of the unity of humanity, equality before the law (*isonomy*), and democracy.

However, here we claim more: practical implications of philosophical discussions are not limited to only politics or morality; they appear in many other fields, including science, technology, and even aesthetics. We return often to this very point, and we wish to dwell on the good implications rather than the bad because they are more interesting and more challenging: bad results are easier to achieve and less interesting than good results.

The History of Epistemology

In a sense, philosophical discussions take place in every culture because almost everywhere people discuss the following and similar questions, which traditionally count as philosophical: How is life maintained? How did it start? What happens after death? What is the good life? What is the good society? How is error to be avoided?

The last question, how can we avoid error, is the toughest of them all. Here, with one exception, all traditions offer the same answer: *follow me closely*. The exception is a Greek tradition and all of its derivatives (including the modern scientific tradition). It broke away from the generally received answer, thus opening the door to what Socrates called philosophy, and more so to what we now call philosophy. (The difference is that Socrates decided to ignore the sciences that were popular in his day – mathematics, astronomy, physics, biology, and many other studies – and centered exclusively on the wish to lead a worthwhile life and to spread the idea that this activity is the most laudable.)

Usually, our culture is identified today as rooted in both ancient Israel and ancient Greece. The Greeks dealt with the following two questions that other cultures rarely discussed except under Greek cultural influences:

1. What are the explanations for what regularly happens in the world? and
2. How can theories be proved?

When discussing the first question, Greek philosophers eventually developed the theory that the physical world consists of four basic elements: earth, water, air, and fire. This theory is not unique to the Hellenic world; indeed, the Chinese also included wood. Either way, this theory is false, as every schoolchild should know. But it is a powerful theory nevertheless; to see its power, consider vegetation. Trees are the products of earth and water; watering the earth is necessary for growing plants; plants wither and then turn back into a type of soil or burn and turn into fire, air, and earth. This was just one theory; many others were present in ancient Greece. Discussions of the questions that these theories came to answer were more common among the Greeks than among other peoples. More than a thousand years after the decline of ancient culture, its heritage gave rise to the diverse modern sciences that have propagated in other cultures with few or no traditional Greek roots. It remains unclear why it is that, of all peoples, only ancient Greece nurtured those who actively sought such explanations.

Historians of culture have recently called the early modern period of Western history "the Renaissance," meaning the rebirth of ancient culture, meaning the wish of thinkers and artists of that period to revive ancient culture. Their chief drive was the wish to revive antiquity on the supposition that the ancient world was superior. The Renaissance thinkers considered great only ancient art and writings on matters religious, philosophical, scientific, and – perhaps most important – political. The revival of the splendor of the ancient Roman Empire was Machiavelli's only motive and the reason for his tremendous popularity that overcame the smear campaign against him – perhaps the worst smear campaign in history.

This craving for ancient glory was not specific to the Renaissance though. The thinkers of the Middle Ages felt the superiority of antiquity even more profoundly, yet they did not expect to do much about it except wait for it with strong yearnings. The Renaissance thinkers had more self-confidence and more readiness to act, so their most important leaders were artists – architects, sculptors, and painters. Their poets and writers were much less influential.

The greater Renaissance thinkers soon discovered that the most important contribution of Greek culture to the world is the idea of intellectual and moral independence: think and do what you think right, not necessarily what your parents and teachers taught you. Exercising independence, they went beyond ancient Greek culture; when the Renaissance was over, it gave way to the Age of Reason. (Historians usually consider the Renaissance to be the period between 1400 and 1600 and the Enlightenment Movement or the Age of Reason to be the period between 1600 and 1800.) In the Age of Reason, science flourished. The philosophical question that engaged thinkers most then was the last of the questions listed at the beginning of this section: How is error to be avoided?

In one sense, this is the question to which every culture devoted much effort. Every culture we know is intent on self-preservation and, it seems obvious, this is only possible if not too many members deviate from the traditional culture. It seems equally obvious that this is possible only if deviation is viewed as error and error is avoided with much investment of energy – in education, preaching, and policing. (In the Middle Ages and more so in the Renaissance, preaching was more effective than policing, and politicians took it very seriously, unlike today, when so many of us consider preaching an empty ritual.) The ancient Greeks were different: they did not think that following one's own tradition is so obviously right. Many of their great thinkers preferred innovation to tradition. (Democritus, the great inventor of atomism, said that to discover a law of nature is better than to be the emperor of Persia.) Then the question arose: Who is a teacher worthy of attention? For clearly, when people disagree, some of them must be in error. Is disagreement necessary, then? Or is it possible to avoid error when presenting interesting ideas?

The field in which this question is discussed is *epistemology*. The word *epistēmē* was translated into Latin as *scientia* and into English as *knowledge* (also, the chiefly Scottish *ken*, as in "beyond my ken," which is akin to the German *kennen*, "to know"). Since Plato and Aristotle, quite a few thinkers – from the time of ancient Greece to the time of Einstein and beyond – viewed science as the set of ideas that is absolutely free of all error. This was the standard view. Is error avoidance at all possible? This question is still under discussion to this day. It is one of the main questions that we discuss in this book.

Whether science in the sense of error-free knowledge exists is still in dispute. This sense is often confused with the sense in which science exists, and it is the business of the science faculty of most modern universities. The confusion amounts to the claim that what the faculties teach is error-free, a claim that has undergone a splendid empirical refutation known as the crisis in physics around 1900. Before the end of the nineteenth century, the view became ever more popular that science is error-free, that scientific knowledge is knowledge proper. This had powerful political implications. Both science and modern industry are peculiar to the West. The conclusion was that the success of industry is due to the success of science so that social and political progress is inevitable. Industrial success made imperialism possible, and the set of ideas that went well with it brought about its philosophical justification: the aim of imperialism was to civilize the whole globe. (The leading imperialist pundit of the time was the writer Rudyard Kipling; he called it "the white man's burden.") But this set of ideas was shattered with the evolution in physics in the early twentieth century. Many physicists then tried to return to religious tradition, as Russell sadly observed. In response, he and other rationalist philosophers said that even if science is not utterly free of error, its ideas are the best because they are the most probable. It is one thing, however, to believe that a certain move in a game leads to good results more often than bad results and another to believe that a certain use of medication leads more often to the gym than to the graveyard (residence in the graveyard lasts too long for the possibility of repeating the procedure afterwards). This leads to interesting consequences, such as the moral dilemma involved in the use of immunization, which rescues millions and kills only a few. Should this return us to imperialism under similar justification? If not, why not? We return to this later in a subsequent chapter.

Error Avoidance and the Foundations of Knowledge

How, then, can one avoid errors? The first and default answer is, follow tradition. It is the oldest and, thus, older than all philosophy. The rejection of this answer is the beginning of philosophy; a philosopher may still decide to follow tradition but not as a matter of course. Most people do follow tradition as a matter of course; they are not philosophers. Another way to avoid error that is still rather simple is to say nothing and do nothing. This was the ideal of many traditions. The expressions of this idea are numerous and they permeate much folk culture everywhere. For example, if words are silver, silence is gold; and, both Chinese and Jewish sages say that inaction is preferable to action whenever possible.

Utter inaction is never possible: the truly inactive is truly dead. The wish to reduce action to a minimum, or the view that it is best, is not very satisfactory either. There is a traditional view that contrasts action with contemplation, and then it seems obvious that contemplation is the better option: many who work hard wish to work a little less so as to have time to observe and think. But this very contrast of action with contemplation is an error. Those who live by it often neither act nor contemplate. Rightly or not, traditional Western culture views research as a valuable form of action. This view and the traditional cultures that follow it all show interest not just in avoiding errors but also in right action, especially in the action of research that increases proper knowledge. We put great value on any explanation of the phenomena around us and in applying these explanations for the betterment of the human condition – and, because we cannot avoid thought and action, we want to do them as best we can. In other words, the epistemological question is: How can we present interesting ideas and act reasonably while avoiding or, at least, minimizing errors? Philosophers often consider this a task for the theory of knowledge, for epistemology.

Epistemology is relevant to the search for theories to explain observed events, especially repeated ones, and similarly to making judgments – practical, moral, political, or aesthetic. We return to this point in the following chapters because, in our opinion, humans are always prone to making mistakes. This idea seems to us so very obvious that we would not have mentioned it, but then we are running against the whole of the tradition of philosophy with almost no exception. The exception is so rare that it has a modern name: the great nineteenth-century American philosopher, Charles Saunders Peirce, christened it *fallibilism*.

It seems that here is an impasse: either we avoid errors and then whatever information or ideas we acquire is knowledge or we are forever ignorant. This is not so. For one thing, it may well be that we live in a world where fate grants knowledge only to those who dare to err. Folk wisdom manifested in innumerable folktales expresses exactly this idea. Or, we may take a risk and acquire information or ideas that may be true but with no guarantee; then the question is: How should we decide whether what we have acquired is the genuine article? These are obvious questions; we meet them regularly in practice. Does epistemology handle them? Does it then offer some practically valuable suggestions?

Because epistemology applies to all human activities, it may be interesting to ask: Where, if anywhere, was its application most obvious? As it happened, its first application was to philosophy, where it naturally was very problematic, and then to geometry, where it was considered the paradigm case.

Geometry has its place in every culture, but in Greek culture it had two characteristics that made it stand out. First, it had axioms and theorems deduced from the axioms, the way geometry is still taught in Western schools two and a half millennia later. It was one of the greatest Greek achievements because it was a case in which thinkers could say that they had overcome human fallibility. Greek geometry rests on the idea of proof, which is the second characteristic that is specifically Greek. To prove a theorem is to show that it logically follows from already proved theorems: whatever follows from what is provable is provable. But this leads to regression: theorem A is provable because it follows from theorems B and C, and B is provable because it follows from D and E, and so on. To stop the regression, some Greek thinker – probably it was Plato – invented the idea of axioms. In his view, an axiom is any simple, self-evident principle, sufficiently obvious to be in no need of proof. This is why Euclidean geometry allows the use of a ruler and a compass only: they are simplest, and the figures that they enable geometers to draw have obvious characteristics. For example, the idea that a straight line – drawn by an ideal ruler – goes on indefinitely in two directions is an axiom of Euclidean geometry. The circle – drawn by an ideal compass – has all points on its circumference equally distant from its center, and that distance is its radius. Many bright high school students find it odd that their teacher ceremoniously tells them something so obvious as a straight line goes to infinity both ways and that a circle has a fixed radius. Teachers try to explain these axioms to these bright students, thereby making things worse, often with the result that the brightest drop out simply because their teacher cannot explain to them what is at stake; the teachers are familiar with the mathematics but not with epistemology. Also, they know how important axioms are for all mathematics, but this is too difficult to explain to students who have no mathematics at all.

Axioms are thus evident but not proven statements, and mathematicians state them in order to deduce from them other statements, thereby proving them. Thus, even if there is no need to state an axiom because it is so obvious, there is a need to state it as part of the mathematical process of proving theorems. Thus, all the theorems of a system follow from its axioms. But, as mentioned previously, the axioms themselves are not amenable to proof and are also in no need of it. This is why, traditionally, they were supposed to be obvious. (The situation in mathematics greatly changed in the nineteenth century.) Their being obvious presumably guarantees that they are true. Is that presumption true? Skeptics pointed at many cases where statements looked very obvious and then someone discovered their refutations, to everybody's satisfaction. Skeptics used such experiences as evidence that no statement is immune. Today, most researchers agree that Einstein showed that Euclidean geometry is not certain because it predicts and explains repeatable observations less accurately than Einstein's own geometry resting on the research of nineteenth-century mathematicians, notably Bernhard Riemann. Historically, doubt about the obviousness of a certain axiom opened the road to modern mathematics, where obviousness is no longer required. This was the famous parallel axiom that states exactly one line is parallel to any other given line and also goes through any given point. Alternative geometries soon appeared that do not obey this axiom. Today, many mathematicians find it hard to explain why tradition viewed the parallel axiom as less obvious than Euclid's other axioms. For example, the axiom that straight lines go to infinity in both directions may seem obvious to people with little training in geometry. Mathematicians say this is not so on a sphere, of course, and a sphere as big as Earth looks so much like a plane. They add that it is not obvious to them that the axioms of spherical geometry are not more obvious than those of plane geometry. However, and more important, they do not care. They study both plane and spherical geometry and ways of correlating them, and they are not concerned with what is obvious and to whom.

Back to our question: How is it possible to avoid errors without blocking the discovery of interesting ideas? Following the example of geometry, for ages, philosophers looked for statements that can function like axioms – that is, statements that are self-evident and can serve as the basis for more knowledge, perhaps even the complete set of axioms that would serve as a basis for all possible knowledge. Although mathematicians gave up the paradigm of this kind of research, there are still many philosophers who seek the self-evident axioms of philosophy.

What are the best axioms for the beginning of any scientific research? There are two alternative answers to this question, they are both very famous, and, as it happens, they are both impervious to any effort to apply them in practice. They are empiricism, the appeal to experience alone, and rationalism, the appeal to obvious abstract assertions alone. This terminology is troublesome because both empiricists and rationalists endorsed rationalism, the theory that states only what we can prove counts. So Kant suggested calling intellectualists the thinkers who rely on some obvious abstract assertions. The empiricists then claimed that the correct starting point for research is a set of reports of what the researchers themselves perceive. For example, "I see now a brown desk." Somehow, this is not sufficiently simple. A desk is wooden, wood is made of God knows what, and there we go. Worse, we see the sun move across the sky, and Copernicus denied that it moves. Soon, the empiricists (John Locke, to be precise) preferred to discuss perceptions that they deemed more immediate, such as "I see now a brown surface." Such statements, empiricists claimed, cannot be wrong, so they can serve as the starting point and the firm basis for knowledge.

The intellectualists suggested another kind of statement as the starting point for knowledge. They claimed that we should start by revealing statements that we cannot imagine as false; that is, we should start not with the senses but rather with the intellect. Mathematicians, we remember, have used this method since Antiquity. For example, how many prime numbers between one and a hundred can be discovered by reasoning alone, without referring to the senses? However, the intellectualists claimed that this method is applicable not only to mathematics but also to statements about the shapes of things in the world. To continue this line of thought, Plato and Descartes said that knowing all about the shapes of things amounts to knowing all about them.

Skeptics need no specific information to object to both empiricism and intellectualism. Empiricism is erroneous, the skeptics claim, because our senses often deceive. If there is a criterion that sifts the true part of the information that the senses convey, then this criterion is imperfect. Moreover, even if we assume that sense *data* (*datum* = given) are certain, as Hume argued, they do not suffice for the construction of sufficient knowledge about anything in the world. Intellectualism is in error, too, the skeptics continue, and for similar reasons: we often err when we reason. If we use a criterion for the reliability of some thinking, as Descartes did when he declared clear and distinct ideas true, then this criterion is imperfect and not even sufficiently clear: What makes an idea sufficiently clear and distinct? Moreover, even if we assume that some (e.g., clear and obvious) ideas are certain, they do not suffice for constructing interesting knowledge about the world. In what follows, we reproduce some of these discussions, stressing the skeptical arguments.

Empiricism, intellectualism, and skepticism were already notorious in Antiquity, in the time of old Greek philosophy. (Old Democritus had a dialogue between the intellect and the sense, in which both parties lost.) At the beginning of the seventeenth century, the renewed discussions became the center of modern Western philosophy. Introductory courses in philosophy, the philosophy of science, or early modern philosophy usually summarize these arguments. However, these presentations tend to ignore the position of the skeptics as much as possible; by contrast, the skeptics occupy center stage in this work.

During the Middle Ages, the question under discussion (i.e., How can we minimize error?) had a simple and generally received answer: to minimize errors, follow tradition, because the Church knows the truth. This is the authority of tradition. In the sixteenth century, the Protestant movement undermined the authority of the traditional Catholic Church. At the beginning of the seventeenth century, Galileo, who was a mathematician and a philosopher as well as a devout Catholic, rebelled against the authority of the Church in matters intellectual and disproved the physics of Aristotle, whose texts university professors considered (almost) as infallible as the Bible. Galileo advocated Copernicus' view that the earth moves around the sun, which is in the center of the universe, and he argued that the moon is not a perfect mirror (it has mountains, valleys, and seas) and that the sun is not perfect (because it has moving dark spots). He then demonstrated by reasoning[2] alone that the speed of freely falling bodies does not depend on their weight – which was another break with Aristotle.

Philosophers then experimented with the idea of minimizing errors and advancing knowledge by the use of both reason and the senses. Intellectualism and empiricism then became the center of the discussion. Unlike the ancient skeptics who were too aloof to seriously discuss the problems that science raises, the modern skeptics approve the use of both the intellect and the senses as a matter of course; however, being skeptics, they insist that neither carries any authority. It is, indeed, the search for an infallible source of knowledge that the intellectualists and the empiricists share, which is precisely the source of their disagreement: there can be no more than one infallible source because two can clash and then one should prevail. Therefore, as intellectualists always stressed, they never opposed the use of observations, but not as the final arbiter. The empiricists were less tolerant: ever since Sir Francis Bacon, they considered the use of theories dangerous unless they are proven, and their proof rests on evidence. Hence, empiricists were opposed to all hypotheses: no matter how tentative one's suggestion of a hypothesis, said Bacon, sooner or later one falls in love with it and then it becomes a dogma and interferes with one's ability to see things as they are, thus disqualifying one as a researcher. This is empiricism, which we discuss later. The two schools share the idea that there can be only one final authority, so the strife between them continues indefinitely, revealing their good faith and keeping skepticism at bay.

Intellectualists suggest that the starting point should be thinking about the substances of the universe. A substance must exist; its nonexistence is unthinkable. In other words, a substance is an entity the

---

[2] The proof is simple: consider two bricks falling together, once as two objects and once as one object (by tying them together, if you insist). You will find conflicting answers to the question: How fast do they fall?

existence of which is provable by rational means. Descartes claimed that the self is such a substance because I cannot imagine myself as not existing: even if I reject all of my views, I am left with my doubts; these are thoughts, and thoughts have a thinker. Just as a property must have an owner and a predicate must have a subject, thoughts have whatever that thinks them, and this item – whatever it is – is a person, and in this case it is the first-person singular, I. This is the idea in Descartes' famous sentence: "I think, therefore I am" – which is a poor translation of his original Latin expression, *cogito ergo sum* – or, more grammatically, "I think, therefore I exist." (The sentence became the slogan of an entire movement, the Enlightenment Movement, to designate the idea that the thoughtless hardly signifies.) However, Descartes' main target was to prove the existence of God. (Although the philosophers opposed the Church as a reliable source of knowledge about nature, almost all of them were religious. The religion that is free of Christianity or any other Bible is deism, as distinct from theism, which relies on some Bible and resides in some religious organization.) God is a necessary substance, philosophers claimed, because – being perfect – He bears all the positive attributes, and *being* is such an attribute (existence of a good thing is nearer to perfection than nonexistence). This is the so-called ontological proof for the existence of God that was already famous in the Middle Ages; modern Western philosophers, including Descartes, Spinoza, and other intellectualists, improved and added to it their interesting elaborations. Immanuel Kant created a great stir when he declared invalid all proofs of the existence of God. He was not an atheist or even a skeptic, however. How he managed this feat is beyond our ability to explain. His refutation of the ontological proof was of great value for logic because he claimed that existence is neither an attribute nor a predicate, which raised the question: What is it, then? This question was one that modern logic attempted to answer. It is still puzzling. But the ontological proof is so obviously invalid: as Russell said, if God exists because He is perfectly good, then so must the devil exist because he is perfectly evil. End of argument.

This is not the only flaw in the intellectualist plan for the construction of knowledge. It is no surprise that it did not succeed. The surprise is that discussions about it were so fruitful and involved revolutions in logic, mathematics, physics, and even biology. The proofs for the existence of God were first to come under severe criticism. Modern logic goes much further by taking all demonstrable statements to be tautologies – that is, statements that are true by virtue of rules of grammar alone, rules that are valid simply because we have stipulated them. Hence, truths in logic are truths by convention, not truths by nature as was intended: no one wants God to exist just because we have agreed to use words and sentences this or that way. Moreover, the assertion that God exists does not lead to any interesting explanation.

The empiricists suggested an alternative. Again, they claimed that direct reports of sense *data*, what is given (*datum* = given) to our senses – being given by Mother Nature – are certainly true. This was Bacon's adoption of a traditional Christian idea to methodology: all errors are due to our willfulness. The given is not due to our doing but to the doing of Mother Nature, so it cannot be faulty. (Here, Mother Nature is God.) Thus, according to Bacon, utter passivity secures freedom from errors. When we sense our *data* in regular associations, we learn that *data* come in regular associations. (This idea played a tremendous role in psychology; it is called *associationism.*) For example, we regularly associate heat sensation in the presence of fire; we conclude that fire and heat come together, and then that fire is the source of heat. This kind of association is *induction*; applying it is *inductive inference.* We can avoid errors, the empiricists claimed, by limiting our thinking to what we can learn by proper induction from proper experience. Experience has to comprise careful observations; induction has to be judicious. What all this means, however, nobody knows, except that both observation and induction must be cautious. How cautious should we be? When we see a smoking gun and a person dropping dead, may we assume that the cause of death is the shooting, or should we wait for the autopsy? If so, then how careful should the autopsy be? And so on.

Hume made all these impossible considerations unnecessary when he refuted the theory by showing that causality is unobservable, no matter how careful our observations. No association, he concluded, can ever be certain. That the sun rose every day until now is thus logically insufficient grounds for the prediction that the sun will rise tomorrow as well. Of course, we do expect that the sun will rise tomorrow, he admitted, and even quite approvingly (we would dismiss him as mad otherwise) but not because past experience logically imposes it. Rather, it is the result of a psychological process that does indeed rest on our observations, but it is psychological, not epistemological. The long and the short of it is this: the prediction that the sun will rise tomorrow is not certain; therefore, it does not have the status of knowledge.

Here, Hume made a strange switch: he cast doubt on the certitude of natural laws and, hence, on their very existence, and then he replaced them with a psychological law on which he could cast just the same doubt. It is thus no surprise that the version of his philosophy that became standard is the extreme skepticism that he found so uncomfortable. That version takes both bodies and minds to be ways of associating *data*: a physical object is the collection of the set of *data* usually associated with a physical object, and a person is the collection of *data* usually associated with a person. On this view, only *data* exist. This is a strange view of that of which the world is composed. However, in the Information Age, certain computer-inspired mechanistic ontologies have lent a certain new cachet to this view.[3]

The next big idea was presented by Kant. He declared the situation scandalous and offered a totally new approach: he found a way to combine intellectualism and empiricism. His trick was to divide the domain among the different authorities so as to prevent all possible clashes among them. His view is thus a compromise or a synthesis: the intellect contributes theories, and the senses contribute informative observation. The ideas that have no observational information with which to combine should forever be doubtful, and the wise should forever suspend judgment on them. Kant did not live by these ideas. For example, theology is a field that is too remote from both experience and scientific theory, so one should suspend judgment in it. Yet, he said that we must assume God's existence. We should overlook this inconsistency of Kant's because it is intricate and irrelevant to the current discussion.

Like the intellectualists and the empiricists before him, Kant also attempted to defeat skepticism. He stated that everything "which bears any manner of resemblance to an hypothesis is to be treated as

---

[3] The *Matrix* movies hammer in this profundity, using yet another variant of the crazy hypothesis about Descartes' demon: we are all parts of a computer game. It is close to Lewis Carroll's comic hypothesis: we are all part of the Red King's dream; when he wakes up, poof we go.

contra-band; it is not to be put up for sale even at the lowest price, but forthwith confiscated, immediately upon detection," and he declared skepticism "the euthanasia of pure reason." Kant claimed that the mind applies its own ways of thinking (its categories) to what the senses receive: this is how we think. Therefore, human knowledge is limited to mere appearances, not to the real, the things-in-themselves. Thus, there is no science from the viewpoint of eternity (to use Spinoza's expression). All discussions of the thing-in-itself belong to metaphysics, a field that is doubtful; hence, it is to be avoided – better to have no metaphysical opinions. Among the contributions of reason, he listed not only the Euclidean theory of space and time and the idea that every event has a cause, he also listed the whole of Newtonian mechanics. He declared these to be the first and last word on their topics. Modern physics takes it for granted that Newtonian mechanics is not the last word and so it does not take Kant's system as the last word either. Newton's theory approximates some better theories and it is hoped that it approximates the truth. Of course, one may suggest other ideas but, as Kant's contemporary, the philosopher Salomon Maimon pointed out, any suggestion about the scientific status of any theory would be another hypothesis, not a necessary truth and, there-fore, neither an item of knowledge nor a proper foundation. Thus, he was the first to draw the heretical conclusion that Newton's theories as well are not certain. His skeptical reading of Kant's structure keeps it intact but not as a foundation, thus undermining the very rationale for Kant's efforts – and irremediably so.

Nevertheless, during the nineteenth century, Kant's influence dom-inated epistemological discussions and brought about some false sense of security. With the crisis of physics in the beginning of the twenti-eth century, severe criticism brought it down. This time, the main attack came with the aid of some powerful developments in logic; declaring scientific truths not truths by nature, critics made it truth by convention and so not final. Indeed, the revolution in physics at the time raised a better alternative to the traditional views about scientific truth. Yet, wishful thinking had its day: the urge to anchor science in solid ground and attain finality won. In response, the logical pos-itivists declared all sentences meaningless unless claims accompany them about the way in which it is possible to verify or refute them by possible empirical observations. For example, a statement like "God exists" is meaningless because there is no way to verify or refute it; and "This desk is brown" comes with the claim that if you doubt it, you can have a look and judge for yourself. Whereas metaphysical utterances are meaningless, the logical positivists declared, scientific theories are verifiable or refutable by empirical observations. Later, they modified their view: scientific statements are also not really certain, they admitted, but merely highly plausible. Scientific theories are, then, generalizations of empirical observations. As long as they meet with no counter-examples, the higher the number of observations that agree with the theory, the higher the probability of the theory.

Under the severe criticism that Russell, Popper, and other philosophers launched against logical positivism, its adherents slowly moved away from the theory of meaning and, finally, shamefacedly relinquished it. Because there are two components to logical positivism – a new one that has to do with meanings and a traditional one that has to do with the foundations of knowledge – the heirs to logical positivism are now mainly concerned with the traditional view of science as probability. This is a premise for a new inductive logic. It is the suggestion that, given a set of *data*, whatever these are, and a set of theories, no matter where they come from, at least in some cases the calculus of probability permits *data* to render one theory most probable, even though not certain. This theory is currently all the rage, despite the refutations that Hume and Popper presented. We review the theory in the next chapter.

A Word about Metaphysics

This study has little to say about metaphysics. This is regrettable, because metaphysics is a major part of traditional philosophy. So much so, that the hostility to philosophy is often taken to be hostility to philosophy as such. This, of course is exaggerated, quite apart from the fact that hostility should have no access to philosophy. Metaphysics is usually considered the theory of the universe, and its major part is ontology, the theory of what there is. Now many physicists are seeking these days the theory of everything, a theory that will offer a full list of the elements of matter and of the forces of nature that should comprise an adequate explanation – whatever this is – of all that we know of the physical universe, perhaps even of the whole universe. This theory would be scientific. A theory was traditionally deemed scientific if it was certain and if it was explanatory. Traditional commentators discussed metaphysics only to the extent that philosophers claimed that it was certain, ignoring the uncertain (the speculative, to use the jargon word) such as all sorts of non-western metaphysics and all sorts of western religious metaphysics (including traditional theology). Yet there was no claim that metaphysics was explanatory. Thus, traditional atomism was deemed not explanatory and thus not scientific; perhaps it was deemed not even certain. As uncertain metaphysics was rejected, the advocates of any general view of the world had to declare their view certain. Thus, two theories of knowledge (epistemologies, to use the jargon word) competed, the one known as the *a priori* or inductive or empirical and the other as the *a posteriori* or deductive or intellectual. Needless to say, as sceptics we reject all claims for certitude, and as modern sceptics we do not reject either method of research, the empirical or the intellectual, and, following Popper we deem each a check on the other.

The traditional metaphysical theories divided all things between two categories, appearance and reality, where descriptions of appearances belong to empirical studies and the description of reality to explain them. This was never achieved. Moreover, the theories about reality were traditionally deemed theories about the one substance or the two substances that the universe really comprises. There is no need here to discuss theories of substance, and one example should suffice: ancient atomism: the world comprises atoms moving in empty space. This raises questions about the atomic structure of anything, from sticks and stones to souls and works of art. Whatever was not considered atomic was dismissed as mere appearances. The doctrine of substance was confused, and lost its popularity among those who respect modern logic, because under its impact it became clear that efforts to reconstruct it are hopeless. Before that, one of the most central questions of modern metaphysics was, are human souls substantial – and so indestructible – or mere appearances? If the soul is real, namely, if it is a substance, is it inherently good or is it inherently evil? Apparently we are capable of good and of bad actions, but the question is not about appearances but about reality. Such questions still engage those who cling to traditional metaphysics as substance theory. They have thus given up the wish to be rational. So one of them declares that the substances that the human soul comprises are fear and boredom; another declares that it comprises fear and nausea. We will ignore all of them and leave the details of rational metaphysics for another day.

2

Skepticism

The Strange Story of the Idea of Error Avoidance

Skeptics have claimed that there is no knowledge, that everything we say is doubtful; hence, error is unavoidable.

Socrates presented himself as a skeptic. By raising questions, he undermined assertions that his peers considered obvious truths. He concluded that one's wisdom rests on the awareness of one's ignorance. His most illustrious disciple was Plato, who founded the Academy and introduced an entrance requirement: one first had to know some mathematics. Plato took mathematics to be true knowledge and the foundation of all other true knowledge, including the political knowledge that is required for the best government. After his death, the Academy returned to the Socratic tradition and was renowned for its skepticism. The philosophers who taught there practiced the method of arguing for and against different answers to given questions and suspended all judgments about which answer is right.

The idea that the suspension of judgment is a virtue became the central teaching of Pyrrho and his followers, the Pyrrhonists. There is no written evidence attesting to Pyrrho's position, but the prevalent view regarding it follows Sextus Empiricus and presents Pyrrhonism as follows. Those who wish to dwell in a peaceful mood (*ataraxia*) should try to argue against every position that they tend to prefer: their view of any question should be as balanced as possible. As a result, they will refrain from assuming any position, and the outcome will be a permanent state of peace of mind. This is a recommendation for a skeptical way of life, in which one neither denies nor asserts any statement about the world. Like all schools of philosophy that seek peace of mind, Pyrrhonism rests on the refuted idea about what brings about peace of mind; whereas, in truth, we still do not know how peace of mind is best achieved.

Sixteenth-century European scholars discovered the writings of Sextus and found his arguments most congenial. Conspicuous among them was Michel Montaigne, who used extant disagreements among scholars as evidence that science is as much a cultural construct as is religion, and proposed approaching it with much doubt. Another was Erasmus of Rotterdam, who used skeptical arguments to attack Luther's doctrine, claiming that we should conform to existing ideas because there is no reliable criterion of truth to apply in efforts to overthrow them, much less replace them by better ones.

Modern philosophy starts at the beginning of the seventeenth century with the ideas of Sir Francis Bacon and René Descartes, who advocated the dismissal of all past opinions without distinction so as to be able to start fresh, thereby achieving true knowledge. Bacon said that unless one totally suspends all judgment about everything, one is unable to investigate nature without bias. After exercising the total suspension of judgment, one can observe accurately and construct science on solid foundations with ease – even in one's spare time.

Descartes accepted Bacon's view of utter skepticism as the starting point of all serious thinking. He practiced this idea of the full suspension of judgment by applying it as methodically as best he knew how. He was no skeptic, but for the sake of reaching the desired certitude, he assumed as extreme a skeptical position as he could imagine. In this process, he evoked the "evil spirit hypothesis." This is the possible hypothesis that all my experiences are creations of an evil spirit that controls all my beliefs and wishes to mislead me. Hence, the reason for my experiences and beliefs is the evil wish of that evil spirit. Later writers simplified this hypothesis; in its simplest version, it is the solipsist hypothesis: all my experiences are misleading because the only thing that really exists is *I* (i.e., the first-person singular, whoever it happens to be) and all the rest is but a figment of my vivid imagination. Some commentators declared this hypothesis a priori very implausible because it is difficult to ascribe to me all the beautiful works of art that come my way and all the intelligent ideas that I have learned. Consequently, the hypothesis has recently reappeared in a new guise as the pictorial idea that possibly all my experiences are misleading, as

I am merely a brain in a vat controlled – perhaps by a computer – and am provided with all the experiences and ideas that I take seriously, being unable to learn that I am a brain in a vat.

Now, let there be no mistake: this hypothesis, in all of its variants, is utterly crazy, and no sane person believes in it or even takes it seriously. Psychologists suspect anyone who does take it seriously or who even thinks one should give it serious attention of a mental imbalance. Indeed, a leading twentieth-century psychotherapist, Ronald Laing, said that Descartes' initial ideas sound suspiciously sick to modern therapists. Thus, all efforts to defend Descartes' hypothesis result from having lost sight of the point of his discussion: there is no need and no possibility to defend a crazy hypothesis. The point is not to believe or disbelieve this or any other crazy idea but rather to *disprove* it (and all of its variants, of course) because any proof of our scientific theories is by itself a disproof of these crazy ideas. Therefore, anyone who claims that extant science is a system of proven ideas should be able to disprove with ease all of these crazy ideas – but no one can.[1] And the crazier the idea, the greater is the insult that its irrefutability presents to epistemology. Immanuel Kant considered this irrefutability the scandal of philosophy (he claimed that he overcame it, but he was just bragging).

In the early twentieth century, G. E. Moore and Ludwig Wittgenstein, the most influential philosophers in England at that time, suggested that only philosophy takes this crazy idea seriously so that philosophy itself is not serious and even pointless. There is no need to disprove crazy ideas, they said, because these are obviously false. Indeed, they are. Moore was forcing his way through an open door, expressing reliance on common sense.[2] Philosophers for centuries

---

[1] The view that science is proven and that physics is scientific amounts to the rejection of solipsism. This assertion was traditionally viewed as expressing a wrong move because the very challenge of solipsism is to disprove the claim that physics is proven. Thus, at stake is not solipsism but rather skepticism.

[2] Young G. E. Moore and Bertrand Russell were under the sway of neo-Hegelianism, Cambridge-style. Appealing to common sense, Moore freed Russell of it and won his gratitude for life. Yet, neo-Hegelianism was not meant to oppose common sense. All modern philosophers, no matter how odd their views were, took common sense for granted, assuming, usually falsely, that their views were commonsensical. And they all, Moore especially, took for granted that common sense is anti-skeptical, despite the famous edict that nothing is certain but death and taxes (Daniel Defoe, Benjamin Franklin). Russell viewed himself as a moderate skeptic bent most on common sense.

taught otherwise because they equated rationality with proof. And, indeed, as Wittgenstein got older, his ideas became less rationalist: he cared less and less about the avoidance of error; instead, he taught that there are only two options: rationality as proof and taking things for granted. Because holding the first option one cannot dismiss crazy ideas as one should, we must take the other, he suggested (but he never said explicitly what his message was). Farewell to doubt and to philosophy. This suited Wittgenstein because he taught that all philosophy but his is sheer confusion. However, Wittgenstein's own writings show him to be mistaken: they cause so much confusion that many who take him seriously invest much effort trying to clarify his texts. We suggest that this effort is a waste of time. The right response to all this is to realize that proof is not possible but some measure of rationality nevertheless is. Hence, both views are erroneous: the view of rationality as proof residing only in science and the traditional Pyrrhonist view that because there is no proof, there is no rationality. They share the identification of rationality with proof. This identification is refuted by the presence of rationality in the absence of proof. Although this is a lesson that Sextus Empiricus emphasized in every page of his great book, he never gave up this identification. Therefore, of course, he could not reject the suggestion to give up philosophy and cling to (present) common sense instead. Thus, Wittgenstein could revive this idea only a century ago. (This is not to speak ill of common sense but rather to suggest that it is common sense that needs outside help for self-renewal.)

Bacon and Descartes, the two great fathers of modernity, were concerned with science, and their efforts were directed toward teaching people to avoid error. They saw human beings as the source of all error and the source of all truth – God or Nature or Reality – the choice among those options depending on one's view of the world. We may err when we speculate, they observed; therefore, we should avoid speculation, they demanded. Thus, in reaching a verdict, a jury should not speculate on a matter about which they have insufficient evidence. This, of course, raises the problem: What evidence is sufficient? The skeptics say none. This denial sounds odd, but many of us use it against capital punishment, and even those who support capital punishment may agree that this denial is not a silly argument against capital punishment although it is a silly argument against punishment as such. And then all who admit that the denial may make sense are skeptics, at least in some legal matters! Both Bacon and Descartes said it is hard to avoid speculation, but it is a must: only then can we be sure that we are free of error because then our ideas are the gift of Mother Nature (Bacon) or God (Descartes) and, hence, they must be true. The hostility toward philosophy is the hostility of speculative metaphysics. (The Latin root of the word *speculate* is the same as that of the word *spectacles*; it designates seeing, meaning the seeing of a visionary, not of a researcher.) It is interesting to realize how much metaphysics went into the views at the root of the traditional anti-metaphysics for which Bacon, Hume, Kant stood.

Hume is the philosopher who is mostly associated with skepticism in the eighteenth century, although he considered this a great injustice to himself – even an insult[3] – because, he said, nothing is easier than the indiscriminate throwing of doubt in all directions. His moderate skepticism was the recognition of the futility of Pyrrho's version of skepticism. He referred to two types of skeptical views: Pyrrhonism, which he rejected, and moderate skepticism, which he embraced, according to which, despite skeptical arguments, our psychology saves us from suspending all belief. Much the way Descartes went about it, Hume also first proved utter doubt and then offered a tool to escape from it. But, whereas Descartes' tool involved mathematics, Hume's involved psychology. He established doubt by arguing forcefully that all beliefs are doubtful except beliefs in immediate experiences because, he argued, there is no rational principle that leads from the certainty of experience to any other certainty (or even probability) of belief in any idea at all. Among the many skeptical arguments that Hume presented, the most famous one refers to induction. To reiterate a previous example, the fact that for eons the sun unfailingly rose every morning is no guarantee that it will rise tomorrow. Therefore, the statement asserting that it will remains in doubt.

Incidentally, most Westerners want science to guarantee tomorrow's sunrise but, to their great chagrin, it tells us that there is some likelihood that the sun will explode instantly. The likelihood is not great, even if we consider not only tomorrow but also, say, the next billion

---

[3] The great Hume was disqualified for a university position because of his alleged skepticism, or so he was informed. He made it clear that he minded the disqualification less than this explanation, viewing it as an insult to his intelligence; skepticism is facile, he said.

years or so. Oddly, science never gave assurance about the sunrise, even though many great researchers (including Laplace, no less) said that it does. But they always were careful to qualify their statements. Their audiences, however, were more than ready to overlook their qualifications.[4] Now, science says, the sun loses tremendous amounts of energy every moment; therefore, sooner or later, it will run out of fuel.[5] And then, even if it goes on rising, it will do us no good. H. G. Wells described this vividly in his science fantasy, *The Time Machine.*

We digress. Hume said he had a way out of skepticism. Unlike most other philosophers, he did not use epistemological arguments to that end. Rather, he claimed that what saves us from the Pyrrhonist trap is the force of psychological processes that make us take for granted what we believe in, regardless of all skeptical deliberations.

To repeat, Hume doubted physics but accepted psychology, which is also quite questionable, of course. Kant made a great effort to avoid psychology. He spoke of the difference between *facts* and judgments and said that epistemology discusses not *facts* but rather the validity of judgments. Yet, he failed: he described the human thinking apparatus and ascribed to it some of the best qualities, such as harmony (which he called "the transcendental unity of the apperception") in assertions that are obviously descriptive – too much so, thus inviting doubt even about the meaning. Thus, the nineteenth-century commentators on his works had great trouble sifting his epistemology from his psychology. This explains why the Humean view of epistemology as a part of psychology is so very popular. It reappears in history in diverse garbs and, at times, also in all nakedness. For example, in the 1930s, an able historian of science, A. N. Meldrum, and more recently also the famous philosopher and historian of science, Thomas S. Kuhn, both declared that the philosophy of discovery is too faltering and should

---

4 Laplace demonstrated that unless some celestial body approaches the solar system, it is stable for at least some thousands of years. Even this doubly qualified proof was refuted a few decades later by a beautiful idea that, after a few more decades, led to the discovery of fractals.

5 The law of conservation of energy is one of the ideas modern physicists are most prone to take for granted. Kant used the law of conservation of energy to argue that this secures the stability of the solar system (because the friction that the tides generate is a loss of gravitational energy). This was ignored, perhaps because it preceded the proofs of Lagrange and Laplace that (contrary to Newton's view) systems that obey Newton's mechanics conserve energy.

give way to the psychology of discovery. In all of its variants, this idea
is psychologism, the view that we cannot help but believe and behave
the way we do and that therefore the explanation of our belief and of
our conduct are inherently parts of psychology.

Hume failed to convince his readers that his skepticism was moderate. Many of them saw him as a skeptic proper, a Pyrrhonist, which still
is the dominant view of him – despite his touching protest – because
he strengthened the traditional Pyrrhonist arguments. This is regrettable because he was of the opinion that sense *data* are certain, so he
obviously was not quite as much a Pyrrhonist as legend says he was.
But that is another story.

Perhaps as the result of the failure of the French Revolution that was
the product of the Enlightenment Movement, irrationalism flourished
in the nineteenth century, especially on German soil, and its adherents offered some crazy metaphysical systems as expressions of their
irrationalism and as a means to undermine science proper. Rationalists could not bring themselves to admit that the irrationalist critique
of rationalism had some value. So, the rise of irrationalism regrettably
pushed the excessive defenders of rationalism to the enhancement of
the traditional hostility to metaphysics, which got a new name: positivism, meaning faith in reason and science, only to the exclusion
of faith in any metaphysics. This made rationalism a kind of political party, one that allied itself regularly to the radical political parties
proper; loyalty to it made discussions of skepticism improper because
skepticism undermines science. This is an error: skepticism and positivism often go together. Indeed, the name of David Hume always
invokes both together, perhaps because his hostility to metaphysics
was brave and systematic. (His positivist ideas about religion appeared
in print only posthumously.)

The great breakthrough came around the middle of the nineteenth
century, in the same period in which positivism flourished: William
Whewell's theory of scientific verification, which was one of the greatest discoveries of psychology ever made. The greatest perhaps was
made by Sir Francis Bacon, who said that our speculations operate as
spectacles: we see the world in accord with them. Hence, whether or
not what we see agrees with our ideas, it looks to us as if they do. This is
now a familiar idea: we refuse to admit cognitive dissonance – that is,

we refuse to admit the very possibility of empirical refutations of our ideas. Hence, said Bacon, better have no ideas to begin with because then what Mother Nature shows is the truth. No, said Whewell: with no ideas, there is no vision at all – what does not enter our *intellectual* horizon is also beyond our *visual* horizon. Many psychologists agree about that and yet they do not see that this is a rejection of the idea that perception is passive. Rather, they often say that we cannot escape the constraints of the intellectual framework of the traditions to which we were born. This is relativism that today the postmodernists have made very popular. It is obviously false because we do learn and we do see new things: otherwise, science would be impossible. Also, some people do change their minds and at times do say so audibly, which Whewell explained by saying that there is a way to defy the disposition to interpret observations as if they agree with our ideas. We develop a new idea, we conclude from it that a special arrangement should give rise to certain new observations, and we test this conclusion. Because we are the source of the idea, it is unlikely to be true. Therefore, our test normally refutes our ideas, so we try again and again. When a test result is positive, we have verified our theory. This is how science progresses, Whewell concluded.

This terrific theory did not appeal to philosophers because it makes the success of scientific research depend on luck. Researchers, however, liked it very much and for the same reason. So, philosophers forgot Whewell and the idea of verification. Scientists did remember it but, in writing history, they forgot its originator. When Whewell's ideas were rediscovered, philosophers were less averse to the idea that research needs luck; therefore, the popularity of positivism increased. However, the idea came too late: in the meantime, Einstein caused a quiet revolution in philosophy. It was rightly in the shadow of his greater revolution in physics; however, in the present study, it concerns us more: Einstein destroyed the equation of error with sin that the scientific tradition unwittingly shared with religious traditions, especially with the religious traditions of the West.

Under Einstein's influence, Karl Popper advocated fallibilism, the view according to which any scientific theory may turn out to be false no matter how well it fits our experience to date. He joined Einstein in claiming that experience may undermine theories or allow for them but never support them in any way. Popper went further and said that to be scientific, even experience has to be tentative.

Our form of skepticism is even more radical: we hold that every statement is doubtful, that information and theories are never certain, plausible, corroborated, or justified – in the philosophical sense of these terms.

Radical Skepticism

Before presenting the arguments for skepticism, we make seven rather technical points, as follows.

First Note

The words *skeptic, skepticism,* and their like have diverse uses. The etymological sense of the words refers to search (*skeptomai = I search*); whether or not this was initially true, it is not true today because it invariably refers to doubt, not to search.

Second Note

Our view that no statement is certain, plausible, corroborated, or otherwise justified refers to the epistemological status of statements. There are cases in which these terms refer to some established or agreed-on procedures and, at times, they make ample sense. For example, laws demanding that certain types of statements should be plausible, corroborated, or otherwise justified before courts would admit them as true. Their demand is that contestants should meet some received standards of plausibility as listed in books of laws of evidence. These procedures do not guarantee the certainty or plausibility that philosophers usually seek: there is no guarantee that these received procedures lead to results that are invariably true, and they often are found to be erroneous. When it seems that a certain kind of error appears repeatedly, legislators try to alter the procedures with the aim of reducing error.[6] They often promise that the reform they advocate

---

[6] The scientific literature often displays confidence in its theories by the claim that they are 99 percent certain. Hence, only one received theory of a hundred is refuted. This is false.

is the last and that after its implementation, the rules become perfectly reliable. How many times should this procedure of reform occur, asked Israeli law professor, Benjamin Akzin, a half-century ago, before we realize that the law cannot be infallible?[7] At times, courts admit false evidence: they still cannot fully guarantee all error avoidance. This is general knowledge: legislators and courts repeatedly try to reduce error by reforming laws of evidence.

Thus, in particular, the cosmetic and the pharmaceutical industries have to test their products. Recently, the U.S. Supreme Court decided that these tests are often too perfunctory; it therefore declared that the tests should be severe, which means that testers should do their best to find fault. It is not easy to demand a manufacturer to seek fault, just as it is difficult to demand that accountants find fault with the data supplied by their employers. But, if a court of law decides that a certain test procedure was not up to the standard and then fines the manufacturer of a defective product for negligence or the accountants for their negligence to report faults, then the scenario looks different. This, too, is not yet a guarantee from any court, and even if there were such a guarantee, it would still be not very efficient because it would not be watertight and not even the best technique is available to avoid error. But, then, no method is perfect, and even if there were a perfect method, we would not know how to identify it; even if we had identified it, we would not know how to implement it with the least amount of distortion.

This is not merely theoretical. Whenever innovation leads to a disaster, inquests or courts may face the question: Was it predictable and thus avoidable?[8] Suppose a test did not eliminate some harmful error. The producers defend their conduct, saying that proper tests failed to disclose the defect. Verdicts then depend on the view of the sincerity, or *good faith*, of the effort of the producers to find the fault in question and the severity of their tests. The jury may have mere common sense

---

[7] Benjamin Akzin, Art. "Legislation: Nature and Functions," in the *International Encyclopedia of the Social Sciences*, 1968.

[8] The Comet-4 disasters of 1954 that were losses of tails during flights, caused by metal fatigue, echo the 1948 novel *No Highway* by Neville Shute, a former aeronautic engineer. The inquest found no negligence because the manufacturer had no reason to take the novel seriously enough to design a test for the failure it had described.

to go by – that is, some unarticulated criteria for sincerity and for severity – but no sooner than it passes the verdict then its procedure will crystallize as articulated criteria, which will be imperfect and invite efforts to improve on these very criteria. This is our conjectural story that may illustrate real-life situations that conform to Popper's philosophy much better than to traditional philosophies – and, of course, it is obviously inherently fallibilist.[9]

The great achievement of the scientific tradition that philosophy could not recognize before the Einsteinian revolution is this: there is no need to justify conduct unless the law requires it, and then the requirement should be specific and depend on standards that have improved through the ages. The same is true for disagreement. The scientific tradition looked askance at it in preference for error avoidance because, clearly, disagreement rests on error: by definition, among several inconsistent answers to a given question, no more than one can be true; therefore, in any dispute, at most, one party may be in the right. Democracy always went with liberalism and disputes, yet its rationality became clear only when Popper rejected the equation of rationality with proof and allowed into philosophy the commonsense idea that some but not all error is rational; some but not all error is due to preventable neglect or impermissible stupidity. (Those who view science as error-free must find all error in research stupid or negligent or prejudiced: error then must be due to some extra-scientific fault.) Hence, Popper's fallibilism is a new version of skepticism. In partial agreement with that of Pyrrho, Popper's skepticism is a denial of the possibility of proof coupled with the new, Einsteinian encouragement to make bold conjectures and put them to a rational test.[10]

In what sense, then, are everyday, commonsense standards of plausibility reasonable? Briefly, they are reasonable as contemporary theories of what seems credible. We return to this discussion in Chapter 3.

---

9 See, for example, E. Shahar, "Popperian Perspective of the Term 'Evidence-Based Medicine'," *Journal of Evaluation in Clinical Practice*, 1997:109–116.

10 The oversight of Karl Popper's theory of rationality may be reasonable (most people are ignorant of it) as long as one uses sheer common sense and does not follow the traditional theory of rationality (perhaps out of sheer ignorance). Popper's theory of rationality is simply the first and, thus far, the only comprehensive alternative to the traditional theory that accords with common sense.

Third Note

The assertion that all statements are doubtful is open to the following two interpretations:

1. No statement is certain or demonstrable.
2. No statement is plausible, corroborated, justified, and so forth (in the epistemological sense of these terms).

We advocate the second interpretation, which is obviously the stronger of the two.

From the days of ancient Greek philosophy to the very end of the nineteenth century, most philosophers understood skepticism along the lines of the first interpretation – namely, that a statement is doubtful as long as it is not certain and there is no certainty. Opposing it, they tried to find what could be known with certainty; however, they could not produce any instance because the skeptics had no trouble dismissing all evidence. (Skepticism, as Hume observed, is very facile.) This made them seek a criterion for certainty; plausibility was not enough of a guarantee for rationality, however. In particular, it is less than religion demands: religious authorities condemn as heretic (if not even downright atheist) the claim that the existence of God is not certain but merely plausible. (This way, Kant made light of the argument from design – the claim that the world's design proves the existence of a designer – the physico-theological proof of the existence of God so-called, although he considered it very strong because, he admitted, it is not clinching.) Some philosophical discussion about plausibility did take place but seldom. The general view was that, according to skepticism, all statements are uncertain even if most people take them for granted.

This interpretation of skepticism ceased to be effective as the result of the discovery that even the best scientific theories are not proven. Tradition deemed scientific only a theory that already has won the honor of having passed successfully the process of empirical test. But any such proof, any proof by successful tests, is merely inductive. Today, philosophers agree that induction from empirical observations cannot possibly reach certainty. We may declare, for example, that all the many observed ravens are black; we may declare that these observations are true, that the ravens seen as black are indeed black. But then even the prediction that the next raven to appear on our horizon will be black does not follow from these declarations. Hence, this prediction is quite uncertain even if its inductive premises are certain.

The discovery that scientific theories cannot be certain, shocking as it was, chimed with the traditional skeptic view that even predictions of tomorrow's sunrise are uncertain. Philosophers soon introduced a new theory of plausibility, just to block the skeptic's claim for obvious victory. This new theory, then, had to justify the familiar faith in tomorrow's sunrise: although it is uncertain, it is beyond reasonable doubt – it is *plausible*; it possesses a high degree of plausibility.[11]

This is the dominant position in contemporary mainstream epistemology. Mainstream philosophers today admit that certainty obtains only in the fields that do not involve experience: logic and mathematics. Mainstream philosophers resist skepticism nonetheless: some statements about our possible empirical experience of the world, such as the prediction that the sun will rise tomorrow, they say, although uncertain in principle, are certain in practice; they are plausible, corroborated, or otherwise justified. This is the most that we can expect science to achieve, they add, demanding that more is unreasonable – and

---

[11] Tomorrow's sunrise was the classical standard example for a justified prediction. It gave way to the color of birds, which is the recent standard example. This is sad because the older example is better. But, all generalizations of observed events (or predictions of their repetitions) are not good enough; assertions about electrons and gene pools are better. Philosophers take the simplest example in the hope of tackling better examples after they overcome the obstacle that the simplest ones pose. This appears to be a sound strategy even though not generally endorsed, however: some philosophers claim that the tougher examples are more suitable from the very start. We do not know how to assess this disagreement because it is between parties, all of whom belong to a school of thought that is not ours. In particular, when disagreements concern strategies, we suggest that if it is at all possible, the right attitude is to be skeptical and try out different ones alternately. (This is what the police do when their list of suspects is challenging.) Although this is possible in much research, in practice it is not always so. Playing chess, one may alternate strategies, but in a chess tournament, one may have no second chance. This is truer in war, where the next battle may bring about an irretrievable loss. And then, skeptics or no skeptics, we all have no idea about which party has chosen the better strategy and we wait with baited breath for Fate to cast her ballot. Science too allows retries but not always. We find fascinating the hope of classical researchers to achieve certainty despite all past failures. We also find fascinating their disappointment at the evening of the classical era, when the hope for retries faded away. This story had immense consequences – social, political, and even military.

the skeptics demand more. Hence, the skeptics are unreasonable (A. J. Ayer).[12]

Note that some versions of fallibilism are stronger than others; our disposition is to advocate a version as strong as we can make it – without becoming unreasonable, of course. To reiterate, fallibilism is the position that any view about the world might be false. It is associated mainly with the philosophies of Peirce and Popper, who stated categorically that no statement about the world is certain. But fallibilism does not entail the logically stronger position, that by itself no statement is plausible, corroborated, or otherwise justified (in the epistemological sense of these terms). And, indeed, Peirce claims that the process of knowledge-seeking reduces doubt. Popper claims less: he asserts that although corroboration by empirical observations cannot make a theory probable, refutation by empirical observations can render it implausible. Although we observe this to be the usual case, and although it is often reasonable, we do not suppose that it is generally the case or that to be reasonable it should be. In this sense, our position is more radical than Peirce's fallibilism and even Popper's.

In what follows, we use the concept of plausibility as a synonym for corroboration and justification. There are, of course, different kinds of justification, but for our purposes we may ignore them; the concept of plausibility represents them all. True, it is always possible to make distinctions and so we, too, can distinguish between the different justificatory concepts; however, it does not serve our present discussion.

Fourth Note

We do not claim that all statements have the same degree of plausibility. Rather, we claim that plausibility (in the epistemological sense of the term) does not apply to statements. We distinguish between the following two positions:

1. Statements can be plausible, but then all statements have the same degree of plausibility.
2. There are no plausible statements, just as there are no magical spells.

---

[12] A. J. Ayer, *The Problem of Knowledge*, Pelican 1956, p. 35.

We agree that the first position is absurd. However, here we are presenting the second position and, in reference to it, we are suggesting that it is consistent and reasonable. Unlike the Pyrrhonists, we are not ascribing the same degree of plausibility to the prediction that the sun will rise tomorrow and to its opposite. Rather, our suggestion is that regardless of what we feel about these two statements, to say that they are more plausible or less is no more than saying that they are more potent or less than spells because the plausibility (in the epistemological sense of the term) of a statement is but a form of the potency of a spell.

Many philosophers who advocate the view that science lends plausibility to its predictions tacitly admit this: they add a principle of induction as the missing item that helps render tomorrow's sunrise plausible, given all past sunrises. The trouble is, no one has managed to formulate this principle sufficiently clearly and in a manner that does not immediately raise unanswerable objections to it. (The same holds for magic.) The traditional wording of it is the principle of the *simplicity of nature*. This or any other wording of the principle should make the future look like the past. But which future? We know that some past events are gone forever, that death is final, that some species are extinct. To know which past events are repeatable and which are not, and under which conditions, is what researchers are trying to find out. It is too much to expect philosophy to wave a magic wand and provide answers to all the tough questions that scientific research has labored so hard for generations to find. Therefore, we suggest that the philosophers who are seeking the principle of induction are doing what is necessary to establish their position, but that this they cannot possibly achieve. Moreover, the reason for which they are trying so hard to find the principle of induction is their wish to justify research and perhaps even to assist it, under the profound conviction that as philosophers, they should not try to replace it. Yet, this is exactly what they are doing, trying to replace research – all quite unwittingly, of course.

Fifth Note

Many discussions in the philosophical literature refer to variants of skepticism that limit it to certain fields. One such example of limited skepticism is the position according to which all scientific theories are doubtful but that there are empirical repeatable observations beyond doubt.[13] (This is the standard empiricist view, and diverse thinkers have advocated it – from Locke in the seventeenth century to Quine in the twentieth.) This kind of skepticism appears as a generalization because it refers to *all* scientific theories, but the generalization itself applies to a limited domain. Not so our position. We assert that, because there is no certainty and no plausibility, the very concepts do not apply to statements by themselves. Nor is there any need for this: we can do without the certainty and without the plausibility that philosophers seek once we see that we can admit that all statements are doubtful and that in admitting this, we lose nothing that is worth keeping. In particular, this does not lead us to the preference of the inaction that the Pyrrhonists and other ancient skeptics advocated.

Hume's skepticism was *almost* total but, contrary to total skepticism, he applied it neither to immediate reports of experience nor to beliefs that rest on simple intuitive logical theorems. On this point, our position differs from Hume's. As previously mentioned, we assert that all statements are doubtful, including reports of immediate experience as well as mathematical and even logical statements. This sounds strange because logic and mathematics are rich with proofs. We do not wish to deny that. We nonetheless assert that the proofs are neither capable of eliminating doubt nor is there any need for this elimination because the doubt that we advocate can do good and do no harm – except when we misread ideas in line with some traditional errors that here we do our best to eliminate.

Sixth Note

It is not our aim to explode as meaningless terms such as *certainty*, *plausibility*, *corroboration*, and *justification*, any more than *spell*; they are meaningful, easily understandable words.

---

[13] We often say that certain ideas are beyond doubt and usually in truth. This sounds like a refutation of skepticism. This is indeed a refutation but rather of the skepticism that Hume rightly deemed facile. We have ample evidence for the assertion that with the advancement of knowledge, the assertion that seems beyond doubt appears as patently false. See the following discussion of nineteenth-century views on sex. See also J. Agassi, *Science in Flux*, 1975, Chapter 51: Imperfect Knowledge.

Many philosophers followed Wittgenstein and tried to resolve (not solve) some insoluble classical philosophical problems by claiming that the terms that necessarily enter the wording of these problems are meaningless or that their wordings are necessarily ungrammatical (not that Wittgenstein and his followers were expert grammarians). We have no wish to take this path. We do not like problems to disappear; we consider sheer magic all play with words that allegedly serve as spells and make them disappear; the magic does not work. People often use sentences in which some terms denote certainty, plausibility, and corroboration or other terms that denote justification. They appear in discussions of some statements, and we do not see how all such extensive use can be dismissed as meaningless without limiting unreasonably our exchanges of ideas.

Wittgenstein declared that he had demolished all philosophical problems by exposing certain words and sentences as devoid of meaning. At first, he referred to meanings in an artificial language of his own making that he deemed ideal (namely, perfect). He was in error, but at least one had to learn his language in order to show this. Later on, he and his disciples applied this idea to natural languages. He then proscribed the literal use of many common words (God forbid) so that it became obvious at once that he was changing the meaning of the word *meaning* without warning and without explaining this change. So, we do not try to fathom it: his proscription is too arbitrary for our taste whatever he exactly meant by the word *meaning*, which we prefer to use in its ordinary meaning or else in accord with its standard use in formal logic – and we take great care to distinguish these two meanings.

Seventh Note

We do not herein refer to probability. We deny the widespread view that it is incumbent on rational people to choose the most probable alternative (to believe in). We also have no use for the probability of statements. The distinction between plausibility and probability, incidentally, is obvious: probability has a well-defined characteristic because it follows the formal calculus of probability; plausibility, whatever exactly it is, does not. What exactly probability means when applied to statements rather than to ensembles of events is unclear and under debate. Consider a generalization such as "all ravens are black." This statement does not describe an event and, although it is possible to assign probability to such a statement, it is not clear which statement is more probable than another, except for a small set of comparisons imposed by the calculus. The calculus declares that the probability of a conjunction is smaller than that of any of its conjuncts. This is clear when the conjuncts are events: it is less probable to throw two sixes in a row (1/36) than to throw one six (1/6). What it means when the two conjuncts are statements is not clear, but at least we can say that if statements have probabilities proper, then the probability of one statement is higher than that of two; therefore, according to Popper, those who want to make only probable statements should say as little as necessary. Such people, he added, are not scientific researchers because they must be adventurous.

Considering probability as frequency is the most obvious application of its calculus. No one knows how to measure the relative frequency of a universal statement, much less how to calculate its probability as a frequency. An interpretation of the calculus of probability exists that assigns probabilities to all statements in any given language. It renders all tautologies most probable and all contradictions most improbable so that no evidence can support or undermine any of them. This reading is very interesting for some purposes but not for the purpose of identifying the plausibility of statements with their probability. By that reading of the calculus, the probability of a universal statement like "all ravens are black" is minimal because the statement refers to infinitely many possible ravens. Singular statements that describe evidence, such as the appearance of black ravens flocking by the drove, do not raise the probability of any universal statement. Of course, if we declare – for example, in the name of the principle of simplicity – that all birds of the same species are the same color, then one instance of a black raven suffices to inform us that all of them are black. But then, all statements involved in this deduction are and will remain doubtful, and most of us will admit that the added premise we just suggested is false (although it holds for some bird species). Still, all is not lost because if instead of speaking of colors we speak of skeletons, then the result is less foolish, at least seemingly so. This shows again that even the simplest scientific deliberations are context-dependent.

The Case of Mathematics and Logic

Traditionally, logic and mathematics were deemed the strongest argument against skepticism: Descartes suggested that even God cannot render $2 + 2 = 4$ untrue. In any case, it was generally recognized that no sane person can seriously doubt arithmetic or geometric truths. The truth of Newtonian mechanics, then, had to follow suit: even though the certainties here are of a different sort, the skeptical doubt concerning them is the same and so it can be dismissed wholesale.

Hume denied that. Our theories are causal and rest on experience, yet causality is not given to experience (= it is in no sense *datum*). Further, the assurance with which geometry is endowed differs from that which accompanies arithmetic because it rests on intuitions that may mislead. All this invites reconsideration because all ascriptions of certitude to perceptions are refuted, and whether we observe causality is an open question. Yet, remarkably, Hume endorsed the received view of logic as unassailable.

Kant revolutionized both logic and mathematics when he offered new arguments to buttress them because he first deprived them of the traditional arguments. He allowed within logic two or three types of formulas (and, presumably, their corollaries): they are the forms **a = a (a is a)** and **ab ⊆ a (ab is a)**, to use modern parlance, as well as all verbal definitions. The latter are true as mere stipulations. He rightly insisted that such definitions add nothing to knowledge (while rightly dismissing definitions as theories in disguise).

The important point is not what Kant allowed but what he excluded from logic to begin with: he declared the truths of arithmetic not a part of logic. This was excessive because he could allow for it by the use of Leibniz's idea that they are verbal definitions. Leibniz suggested that $1 + 1 = 2$ is not an equation but rather a definition of the word 2, so that spelling out $2 + 2 = 4$, we get $1 + 1 + 1 + 1 = 4$, which, likewise, is not an equation but a definition of the word 4. (Leibniz's idea was revived and updated by Alfred Tarski.) It is hard to know whether Kant deemed the truths of arithmetic at that stage more or less doubtful than the axioms of Euclidean geometry or even those of Newtonian mechanics. His concern was to move to the next stage and offer a new justification for them, and his intent was to elaborate on that stage. He therefore lumped them all together and called them by the fancy name of transcendental logic, which he defended at length. His defense is pointless because transcendental logic is not logic at all; he never attempted to explain why he called this cluster of transcendental assertions a logic except to say that they are all beyond doubt. This is obviously flimsy. (Hegel soon followed suit: he declared as logic all the fancy pronouncements that he decreed, thus identifying with logic not only the allegedly certain but also the allegedly true.) Still, Kant's hardly argued opinion about the status of certain theories led to huge changes: the search for their refutations. A new geometry and a new logic thus emerged. Geometers first omitted some of Euclid's axioms and then they got more daring and examined all sorts of non-Euclidean alternatives. The concluding point of this process was Einstein's dissent from Kant that is the consensus today: inasmuch as geometry is about the world, it is not certain, and inasmuch as it is certain, it is not about the world. We dare to go further: even if it is not about the world, we propose, geometry is not certain. No assertion is.

The quest for certainty led Kant's critics to the study of the foundations of mathematics. Georg Cantor (who was contemptuous of him) managed to present arithmetic as a part of abstract set theory. Gottlob Frege developed a new logic to show that set theory is a part of logic; Russell followed suit. Their theory is known as logicism, which today is taught as the last word, even though it was refuted by Russell and more thoroughly by Quine.

Prior to that theory, David Hilbert developed the revolutionary idea that the axioms of a mathematical system are definitions of sorts: they define or characterize that system. Thus, the axioms of Euclidean geometry are true by the convention of seeing them as characterizing a system; they are truths by convention: we call Euclidean any system that abides by Euclid's axioms.

Thus, mathematical truths are unassailable as parts of logic or by definition. Does this invite further justifications for them? We do not know. Frege and Russell did offer one: they deemed logic a characteristic of the ideal language. Today, logicians no longer entertain the view that an ideal language is possible: they deem all languages conventional. And so, it seems, Hilbert's view prevails. Why then endorse the conventions that mathematics offers? Hilbert was more intent on defending his view that the conventions are commendable than on explaining why they are (he found this unnecessary). The question, then, is: Do the truths of logic possess greater force than those of mathematics? If not, are alternative systems of logic possible akin to the alternative possible systems of geometry? And, if yes, do these create alternative systems of arithmetic? These questions engaged many thinkers in the twentieth century and led to exciting results, some by Hilbert's former students and some by his critics.

Enter Imre Lakatos. He presented the history of mathematics – only snippets, to be precise – as that of trial and error. He convinced Popper that mathematics is as much a series of conjectures and refutations as science is. Popper still kept logic apart: he, and more so Quine, took the demand to eliminate contradictions as more than a mere convention: if anyone allows for them, said Quine, then one thereby shows oneself to be confused or else using words in a totally new and different way. Popper went further. He developed a version of logic (called natural deduction) that presents it as a set of rules of inference. He showed that different systems of logic simply follow different sets of rules of inference, and he opted for the one that is strongest because it is the best tool for the elimination of errors.

The numerous varieties of reasonable claims for truths and more so of ways to elaborate on these claims, contrary to received impressions, are agreeable to skepticism because, clearly, none is assuredly error-free and none is in need for such assurance: taking some of these truth claims seriously, we suggest, invites their careful examination. We suggest that skepticism encourages taking them seriously; perhaps they are possible at all only after skepticism is admitted.

Let us conclude this outline by opening one such discussion. What exactly is a truth by convention? Who are the people who convene and how do they convene? What are their aims? Are there better conventions to further these? In particular, no one can show that the Socratic search for contradictions and the efforts to eliminate them are the best tools in the search for the truth. The progress of logic and of mathematics in the last two centuries is tremendous, and it did overthrow many ideas that were deemed indisputable truths, culminating with Popper's overthrow of the equation of rationality with certitude. It is consequently becoming increasingly easier to be skeptical if not also increasingly imperative.[14]

---

[14] A similar case concerns doubt being easy to raise only in general, not in detail. Thus, to say in principle that Newton's theory is not certain is not very helpful. Showing that it is replaceable is better, but it was so difficult that it had to be done with

The Skeptical Arguments

Skeptics have raised two kinds of argument against the claim that certitude is attainable. One is general and has already been mentioned: a statement is certain or justified if it is proved, but proof is impossible because it is question-begging – any criterion for the validity of a proof requires a different proof (because self-validation is too easy and always possible and therefore leads one anywhere one likes; hence, it is useless). A justification procedure invites a justification for itself and so on *ad infinitum*; hence, no justification is final. For example, character witnesses are possibly unreliable and then, for their testimony to be acceptable, they need character witnesses to testify that they are reliable, and so on until we exhaust the population.

The arguments of the second kind are specific: they are counterexamples against each presentation of an allegedly reliable source of knowledge. Lord Acton was a Roman Catholic, yet he found intolerable the idea that the Pope is infallible, saying that this grants him absolute power and absolute power corrupts absolutely. We sympathize but try to hold even this wise adage in doubt. We go further and say that no number of convincing arguments can prove that our skepticism is true; rather, they disprove instances for the opposite view, the view that proof is somehow attainable.

As it happens, today – when most philosophers still combat skepticism any way they can – almost all of them still view only empiricism as a serious contender for a theory of the attainability of certitude (the rest of them retry Kant's way). So, nowadays, the presentations of alternatives to skepticism refer mainly to variants of empiricism. This is the view that knowledge comprises what we perceive and what we infer from what we perceive by diverse means, deductive and inductive, *and nothing more*. These two assumptions are exactly what Hume referred to in his proof of the impossibility of induction. Latter-day efforts to refute him rest on innovative ideas about both perception and inductive inference. (Deductive inferences stand

some success first. It is in this sense that – his general skepticism notwithstanding – Einstein spoke of a specific part of physics (i.e., thermodynamics) as relatively certain. Even that was more certain in general terms (the phenomenological theory) than in detail (the statistical theory) that he managed to have replaced (by the Bose Einstein statistics).

apart simply because they are not under debate in this context.) No one knows exactly what perception and inductive inference are, much less which perception is reliable and which inductive inference is acceptable. Still, broadly speaking, we know what together they are supposed or hoped to do: they should lead from empirical observations to generalizations and other theories without allowing error to creep in or, at least, while reducing significantly the rate of scientific error.

Discussions of perceptions should refer to empirical studies, to the field of study known as psychophysics. The pioneers in this field were hoping to illustrate Kant's idea about observation reports as the outcome of the application of theory to observation. It is doubtful that this can be done, but it was possible to refute some specific simple theories, those that are definitely no longer endorsed in up-to-date science but are still extant in the philosophical literature as a sort of fossil. Specifically, it is easy to refute the specific empiricist naïve theory of perception that Locke and Hume espoused and that most empiricist philosophers still piously uphold in a sincere effort to find cases of error-free perceptions. Thus, these efforts assure that they are steeped in error. They proceed regardless of the empirical refutations of their views in search of inductive inferences that rest on what is directly perceived; although what it is that is directly perceived, no one knows – except that it is not what Locke and Hume said it is and that it should be error-free. However, just because of this last characterization of what is directly perceived, we suggest that looking for it is a wild goose chase.

For our part, although we are quite ready to take psychophysics seriously, we do not need it as a source of skeptical arguments. We consider the ancient classical arguments against the reliability of what we perceive – directly or not, as you like it – both interesting and sufficient. Yet, as it happens, the best presentations of these lovely ancient arguments are now in the psychophysical literature. Anyone interested in this can consult a modern textbook on perceptions or, better yet, visit a psychological laboratory.[15]

---

[15] Almost all universities house psychophysical laboratories, and most experiments that they illustrate come from the traditional psychophysical literature and its criticism of the traditional empiricist perception theory. The power of these experiments indicates the great hold that the classical perception theory still has on us.

So much for the arguments about perception, classical and modern; the next issue for the defenders of empiricism is induction.[16] Now, whatever exactly induction is, a prolific philosophical discussion about it is taking place in an attempt to dispel the refutations of induction, misnamed as the paradoxes of induction, which seriously undermines the very idea of induction as a means for tapping the source of our knowledge. The endorsement of the refutations of all extant theories of induction (or of all versions of the theory) is permissible even though uncomfortable, as long as the insistence that learning from experience by induction is nevertheless quite possible accompanies it, and that once we show this, we can also vindicate induction. The discomfort just mentioned is due to the inability to explain why no study of induction by inductive means takes place. Such a study may fail to vindicate induction; nevertheless, for inductivists, it is worthwhile because it will elicit the theory of induction that they wish to vindicate. In truth, however, this is impossible because real science is fallible and induction is supposed to prevent error or, at least, reduce it significantly. Even if certitude is replaced by some surrogate, that surrogate is supposed to reduce error as well as possible, thereby providing a surrogate infallibility, which likewise cannot be found in the real world. If any induction is clear, it is that like in the past, future philosophers will fail to exemplify valid induction, much less to vindicate it. But let us leave this discussion and report the paradoxes or, rather, the most famous of them.

One famous paradox of induction is attributed to Nelson Goodman and it is as follows: Let us arbitrarily choose some date in the future – for example, the year 2100 – and define a color "grue" (i.e., a hybrid of "green" and "blue") such that an object is grue if and only if it is green until 2100 and blue thereafter. Now, consider the following two statements:

1. All emeralds are green.
2. All emeralds are grue.

---

[16] The problem of induction may be worded thusly: What generalization is acceptable? Nelson Goodman, whose ideas are discussed herein, proposed that generalizations are acceptable if and only if they are projections. This solution of the problem of induction raised the problem of projection: What generalization is a projection? After a few decades, his proposal and all ensuing discussions mercifully sank into oblivion.

By any theory of inductive support, available empirical evidence supports or undermines both statements equally because whatever evidence supports or undermines the one supports or undermines the other for the very same reasons, whatever they may be. This is no surprise because Goodman devised the predicate "grue" artificially and solely to meet that end. And, because "grue" is artificial, we can replace it with any other hybrid term, and so find that the evidence about colors of emeralds in the past does not favor their present color any more than any other. This example is only a sophisticated demonstration of the idea that Hume proved: there is no valid inference from past events alone to any conclusion about any future events. Those who take Hume's argument seriously do not need Goodman's; the latter made waves only because it makes more conspicuous the hopelessness of efforts to get around Hume's proof. But, for those who do need such conspicuous examples, there are some that are much easier to follow, like those developed earlier by Russell: all events are observable, or all events happen prior to the current date.

Yet, there is a reason for the success of Goodman's paradox. It is in its being a (redundant) critique of a specific, popular theory of induction – that induction rests on simplicity. Thus, "all emeralds are green" is simpler than "all emeralds are green or blue," and the simpler competitor pushes the less simple one out of the ring when they compete for the title of the empirically most supported theory. Goodman merely created a new predicate that renders a deplorably complicated theory apparently and respectably simple. Of course, the artificiality of "grue" is deplorable; Goodman himself agreed to that. But he looked in vain for a reason to dismiss "all emeralds are grue." The artificiality of "grue" is insufficient reason, he said, because many respectable predicates that science uses regularly are also artificial. The arbitrariness of this predicate is objectionable, but the motive for the suggestion of a new term is irrelevant: like clues that detectives can employ, it should lead to better arguments, to ones that can stand up in court. The detectives are still working on it because they are convinced that the suspect – Hume's proof – is guilty as charged, that induction is alive and well, and that therefore Hume's proof is somehow invalid. The way they go about it is their effort to refute Goodman's paradox. No one has yet found any new satisfactory resolution to this paradox. Until they do, we must leave them to their toil.

Another famous refutation of induction is the paradox of confirmation (so-called) of Carl G. Hempel. His is somewhat earlier and somewhat less general than Goodman's because it rests on the very popular hypothesis that whatever inductive inference is, it involves the validation of general laws by their observed instances, via corroboration. This is known as the theory of induction from instances or confirmation by instantiation. For example, because a black raven is an instance of the general law that "all ravens are black," any observation of a black raven at any time and in any place is supposed to confirm the law. Likewise, the same theory of instantiation implies that every observation of a non-black non-raven confirms the general law that "everything non-black is a non-raven." Now, a white shoe is non-black; it is also a non-raven. Hence, by the theory of instantiation, every observation of a white shoe confirms the general law that "every non-black thing is a non-raven." Further, the two statements in question are logically equivalent: of necessity, "all ravens are black" is true if – and only if – the statement "every non-black thing is a non-raven" is true. (This is the famous law of classical logic called the law of contraposition: "all S are P" is equivalent to "all non-P are non-S.") Hence, an observation of a white shoe – that is, an observation of anything at all except for a non-black raven – confirms the theory that "all ravens are black." Thus, every observation whatsoever either agrees or conflicts with every theory.[17] This sounds absurd because we naturally judge most observations irrelevant to any given theory; that is, almost any observation is utterly indifferent to the choice between a given theory and its negation. Hence, the theory of induction by instantiation is false. Yet, Hempel's refutation is not taken any more seriously than Hume's; therefore, he called it not a refutation but rather a paradox. And this is how it is seen quite generally (which, alas, is indicative of the state of the art).

Hempel tried to cope with his paradox, to resolve it, to show why it only looks strange but is not really. It is clear why he wanted to do away with it: he was convinced that induction by instantiation is right. He

[17] In 1935, Popper suggested that every scientific theory should be stated as a negative existential statement: "in no space-time region is there an x" where x is what the theory forbids. Because most space-time regions are empty, any scientific theory is amply instantiated. Hence, said Popper, confirmations for any theory are for the asking; it is tests of good theories that are difficult to devise.

offered two excuses for the paradox. One is that in choosing between two competing theories (e.g., "all ravens are black" and "all ravens are blue"), we deem irrelevant any item (e.g., "this is a white shoe") that supports both equally. The other is that the support that seems to us paradoxical is too small to matter. Now, the first excuse is questionable. Whenever there is a tie, we want to know about it because we may seek a change in the satiation that would break the tie. In the present case, we may not care about this because the contribution of the evidence is too small; that is, the first argument relies on the second. As to the second argument, that the quantity of support that some allegedly relevant data lend a given hypothesis is too small to matter, the idea that support is quantitative, is not one that Hempel studied; he simply pulled it out of the hat hoping that it would make the paradox vanish. It does not, and it raises more paradoxes, as we show when we discuss the quantitative theory of support, typically called inductive logic or the theory of probability of hypotheses.

No one has found any satisfactory argument to make Hempel's paradox go away and no one noted that Hume's initial criticism of induction is aimed at induction by instantiation.

Russell, although an inductivist, rejected induction by instantiation. He had a nicer refutation than Hempel of the view that a theory is supported in the presence of instances for it and in the absence of instances contrary to it. Take any theory and extend the class of which it speaks in any way that dodges meeting counter-instances (by including, say, all elementary particles) and (because elementary particles are colorless) you have added confirmations for free. Of course, it is strange to add any items to a given class just to have a better confirmation. But how do we legitimate any definition of any class? Modern logic says that all such classes are equally legitimate. Yet, inductivists such as Goodman feel that some classes are more natural than others and if we knew why, we would solve the problem of induction. A whole vast literature is devoted to this matter, the so-called study of natural classification. That study is doomed to failure because what is natural either rests on a theory, and that theory may be false, or else it may rest on intuitions; even some of the best naturalists have changed their views. Of course, the way out may be to prove the theory of natural classification by induction. But because the search for the proper principle of induction depends on the search for the right principle of natural classification, this move is disqualified.[18]

A third argument against induction refers to *ad hoc changes of theories*. The Latin word means "for this" and it applies to all changes that fit the need for change without examining the possibility that perhaps a bigger change is needed. This method is repeatedly used in law courts because judges should not legislate, but at times they simply cannot apply a law where its application makes no sense. So, in such cases, they have few options but to make exceptions, and they make them as narrowly as possible, sometimes while pleading with legislatures to reform the law – not ad hoc, but radically. Ad hoc changes of theories work as follows. Suppose some people share the prejudice against Ruritanians and honestly consider all of them stupid. Later on, they bump into a wise Ruritanian, Tom. Consequently, they change their view and assert that all Ruritanians but Tom are stupid. They bump into another wise Ruritanian, Dick. Consequently, they change their view again and make exceptions for both Tom and Dick. Thus, they go on changing their view whenever they find a counter-example to their prejudice. Such changes are ad hoc, and a theory that one alters to encompass corrections ad hoc is an increasingly ad hoc theory. Credence in it diminishes, they say, but the rules of induction allow for it: according to them, nothing is wrong with ad hoc changes. By these rules, all the necessary ad hoc modifications to the theory are welcome: they should not reduce support for it.

A fourth argument refers to the status of *simple* theories. Consider the presentation of at least three measurements of two parameters A and B on a grid that appear as if they more or less form a straight line. We tend to see a straight line going through the points.

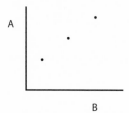

A

B

---

[18] Goodman suggested that what characterizes a proper (i.e., "natural") class is the ability to generalize assertions about its members, a quality that he calls projectibility (*Facts, Fiction, and Forecasts*, 1954).

This line is not there: the conclusion that the data are on a straight line does not follow from the observed points because there are infinitely many ways to draw a line through them (e.g., an infinite number of wave functions that coincide with these points). The conclusion that the correct line is straight, then, is an extrapolation. All extrapolations raise the same difficulty for the empiricists: it is our old acquaintance, the problem of induction. This problem blocks the way to any explanation of the preference for the linear function over each of the countless other functions that fit the same data. Some empiricists have tried to solve the problem by means of some criterion of simplicity. We may, of course, consider tentatively the hypothesis that linear functions are the simplest, and perhaps also the hypothesis that as such, they are the best explanations. This quickly leads us to two questions: By which criterion of simplicity do we judge the straight line the simplest line? Why is the simplest theory preferred and in what sense? Many empiricists have tried to answer these questions but, as far as we know, they despondently admit that none of the answers that they know stands up to the most obvious criticism. They still are optimistically convinced that a simple and obvious answer evades them, although it is simple and obvious that they are looking for a foolproof method which is but a pipe dream. (Also, the need for a foolproof method to sustain one's optimism hardly seems so optimistic.[19])

A similar analysis applies to what is known as Occam's razor, which is the demand to eliminate unnecessary entities. It possibly includes the demand for simplicity and possibly a special case; this, in turn, depends on what we consider unnecessary under which conditions. Consider the following situation. Wanting to know what makes some substances combustible, Stahl stated that combustibles can emit large quantities of phlogiston (*phlox* is Greek for *flame*), which they do as they burn. Lavoisier then said that combustibles can absorb large quantities of oxygen, which they do as they burn. For a time, there was evidence against the older theory and none against the new one.

---

[19] The story goes on, of course. Some laws are expressed as functions that are not linear. For example, they may be logarithmic. If we use logarithmic scales, the logarithmic function becomes linear. If this sounds odd, let us notice that on logarithmic scales, linear functions do not look linear. The very choice of coordinates thus expresses a theoretical bias. The same holds for the empty pages of music sheets because the sets of five lines refer to Western scales.

Nevertheless, some people found it difficult to let phlogiston go. They could, of course, consider Lavoisier's theory true, give up any refuted assertion about phlogiston, but still insist that, while absorbing oxygen, combustibles also emit phlogiston. Most of us consider this idea silly; it is name-calling, not an argument. We present this idea as a challenge to explain or disregard the feeling that this idea is stupid. Many meet this challenge by asserting that Occam's razor should shave off this remnant of an outdated theory because it is quite superfluous. Admitting this, we may ask: Is Occam's razor a part of the principles of empiricism and induction? Does it even chime with them? Empiricists have failed to show that it does, and Popper showed that the two are in conflict: the more unnecessary entities we admit, the more we will be prepared to meet events that do not fit our present ideas about the world. However, ignoring Popper's critique, we can still ask: Is Occam's razor not superfluous? If it is, should we not throw it away?

Finally, a fifth argument against induction rests on the difference between prediction and explanation. Consider a theory and the observations that conform thereto (an observation conforms to a theory if it is an instance of a generalization that follows from said theory). Does it matter which comes first? Most advocates of traditional empiricism follow Keynes's assertion that because credibility, plausibility, or probability is a logical relation between theory and observation, the time sequence in which they appear should make no difference. They are all aware that a theory that yields a prediction that is confirmed seems thereby more convincing than the explanation of already known observations. The majority of advocates of traditional empiricism deem just such persuasiveness to be an illusion of presentation. But skeptics view the difference as another entirely salient refutation of traditional empiricism. Both explanations of observed phenomena and prediction of new results are hypothetical, but all the more so, prediction affords experimental tests of hypotheses, not random unbiased observations toward induction.

These are some of the main arguments that refute traditional empiricism. They do not prove that skepticism is true; rather, they refute the given empiricist answers to skepticism. They do not refute all versions of empiricism, especially not those versions (if any) that are fallibilist. As to the claim that there is a possibility of newer and better arguments against skepticism, it is a general claim and it invites a response that must be general as well. We have already discussed this and are only going around in circles, as we have in philosophy for the last two or three centuries – all because of the refusal to abandon traditional empiricism and perhaps re-embrace it in some fallibilist version or seek such a version if none is available.

The traditional refusal to abandon traditional empiricism is very strong. There is a strong argument in its favor: we do learn from experience. Now, skeptics need not deny the possibility of learning from experience; they deny that progress is due to error avoidance and they deny that it leads to certain or even plausible results. To reiterate, the call for error avoidance is but a call for inaction. Learning from experience is wonderful but, by being a human activity, it is risky; it is not error-free. What is objectionable in traditional empiricism is the demand to limit one's beliefs to justified ideas. This demand seems to make a lot of sense. But then, justification is either error-free and therefore impossible or prone to error so it is useless for the traditional empiricist ends. Worse than that: empiricists cannot justify their view that skepticism is false; so, by their own standard, they should not oppose it even if they may insist on not endorsing it. But, the suspension of judgment about the suspension of judgment is itself a suspension of judgment. This sounds clever, but it is merely a roundabout way to say that skepticism is trivial. It sounds perverse because some skeptics – Pyrrho and his followers – have appended to the trivial thesis the perverse idea that action should not rest on doubtful ideas. The following section discusses this in some detail.

Skepticism in Epistemology

Skepticism was never popular in the West. By the traditionally popular view, skepticism is just a teaser; it comprises an assault on rationality and even on plain common sense, a kind of conjurer's trick. No matter how clever and convincing conjurers can be, no sane audiences will fall for them, except that conjurers please their audiences when they tease their imagination. Skeptics do not please their opponents, who try hard to find the skeptic's sleight of hand but have failed to do so for centuries. And any competent and honorable debunker of conjurers might have conceded that much by now! Contrary to the popular view, then, we repeatedly advocate the skeptical view as outlined herein, claiming as straight-forward, rational, and common sensical that there simply is no way to guarantee that any discourse can ever be certain or plausible in the epistemological sense of these concepts.[20] It is easy to show the difference between the two senses of plausibility – the epistemological and the common: only the former claims infallibility (in some sense or another); common sense rests on commonly shared suppositions that admittedly may be false. We have little to say about common sense, being that it is such a little studied field.[21]

The view that skepticism in epistemology is absurd and a conjurer's trick rests on the mistaken idea that it entails the following conclusions:

1. Skepticism is objectionable because the assertion that every statement is doubtful condemns itself as doubtful. In this sense, skepticism is inconsistent.

2. Skepticism blocks the adoption of any view and any mode of conduct: it prevents its adherents from saying why they believe that the sun will rise tomorrow and why they prefer the elevator over the window for exiting from the top floor of a high-rise building.

3. Skepticism blocks all reasonable accounts of the progress of science and of common views about the world (e.g., the superiority of the views of experts over those of the ignorant or the views of the sane over those of the insane).

Now skeptics can easily parry these attacks, even though possibly not the traditional skeptics of the Pyrrhonist persuasion.

---

[20] See Joseph Agassi and J. R. Wettersten, "The Philosophy of Commonsense," *Philosophia*, 1987, 17:421–437. See also Joseph Agassi, *Science in Flux*, 1975, Chapter 15, Imperfect Knowledge, and *Science and Culture*, 2003, Chapter 5.4, Science and Commonsense.

[21] The motive for the development of famous schools of commonsense philosophy, both the Scottish and the twentieth century, was a response to skepticism. A skeptical commonsense philosophy is still absent. See J. Agassi and J. R. Wettersten, "The Philosophy of Commonsense," *Philosophia*, 17, 1987, 421–437.

The first of these assertions is confusion between truth and certitude. Skeptics consider every statement doubtful, not false: some truths are obviously doubtful. Take the different bets in a given horse race. Obviously, all of the horses are uncertain and only one will be the winner. Here is a simpler argument. Consider any conjecture; if it is not true, then its negation is. Yet, both are doubtful. Hence, some true statements are doubtful. Skepticism is too, we contend. The discomfort that doubtful truths cause for some people, we suggest, is due to dogmatic education.

The second assertion rests on the false assumption that views are open to choice, that they abide by decisions. Indeed, confusingly enough, the very term *decision making* may even be used to mean drawing conclusions: decision theory rests on the idea that (in principle) a computer fed with the right information (about our psychological composition and circumstances) can decide for us better than we can. But, as Robert Boyle, Charles Saunders Peirce, and George Orwell[22] asserted and as Benedict Spinoza and David Hume argued at length, beliefs are given. One cannot choose to believe that the sun will not rise tomorrow. And, because skeptics are at liberty to assume (tentatively, of course) that beliefs partake in the determination of conduct, they need not assume that the choice of a mode of conduct is arbitrary. We return to the psychological theory of the change of belief in the next chapter.

Contrary to the third assertion, skeptics may resort to common sense. Their critics do not have this right because common sense takes much for granted with no proof. Otherwise, common sense could never prove erroneous as occasionally it has. Thus, skeptics may explain scientific progress as a process of evolution. The superiority of the expert and the sane over the ignorant, the dogmatist, and the insane rests on the ability of the former to criticize the errors of the latter and, at times, to also point out options that they omit or ignore. In particular, at times skeptics criticize and improve the standards of criticism in specialized contexts. Indeed, the great skeptic historian, Armando Momigliano, suggested that all the improvements

---

[22] Robert Boyle, *Occasional Reflections* (Sec. 4, Disc. xi); George Orwell, *A Clergyman's Daughter*, toward the end of the novel. Peirce said this in a private letter to William James.

of standards of scholarship that historians regularly employ today are the product of skeptical historians of the relatively recent past.

Practical Implications

Let us consider cases in which we are asked to justify views or actions. Usually, when a view is considered true, the demand to justify it does not arise. The idea that it is considered true due to its justification is plainly false because too many views are received despite obvious criticism. We are usually not asked to justify errors that have led to successful actions. Mark Twain told the story of a commander who confused right and left so he made his soldiers meet head-on an ambush that was meant to hit them from behind; he won a medal. We are usually asked to justify errors that have led to disaster because we are accountable and must show that the disaster was not due to negligence. For example, commanders consult subordinates and ask for criticism of their plans. If the commanders reject the criticism with disastrous results, they must subsequently justify that rejection, which is not always easy.

Empiricism had a profound influence on our culture and mainly but not all to the good. Most reasonable and responsible people try to avoid error, but when they do err, they regrettably try to hide it because they do not like to admit it because empiricism says that their errors were avoidable. It relieves the tension all around to admit that even though, in most cases, the effort to avoid error is obviously laudable, the hope to completely succeed is plainly harmful. This is so because it puts excessive demands on everyone and thus makes all of us foolish and irresponsible every time we err, even though we all agree that some of us are wiser and more responsible than others. (As previously mentioned, one of the standard anti-skeptical allegations is that skepticism precludes the distinction between the judicious and the foolish, between the sane and the insane; the shoe is on the other foot.)

Few intellectuals find unsatisfactory theories that they had publicly declared satisfactory, especially if they are their own, and fewer are then ready to withdraw them openly and clearly. Even fewer intellectuals admit that this is the outcome of some justified criticism of their opponents. Most of the few who have admitted mistakes declared that they changed their mind following their own criticism. The admission of having made a mistake is still considered self-humiliation of a sort, and the admission that this was forced by others seems worse.

Politicians, to mention an obviously worse example, regularly try to steer clear of refutations by presenting views that they hope no one can refute. Instead of presenting any cogent political platform as, for example, in suggesting a detailed plan about how to reduce poverty, they only declare the intention to do so or to apply new social policies – but they do not specify which novelties they intend to introduce, much less how they could help – keeping their claims impossible to refute. This, then, implies a practical suggestion: when politicians present their ideas and plans, concerned citizens should not attempt to criticize them because it is futile; rather, they should insist on demanding some refutable ideas. This way, if their ideas turn out to be false, we may hope to be able to seek new plans for improvement, demand governments to adopt them, and, if need be, elect new candidates to office.

Philosophers habitually apply similar strategies. They reduce possibilities of being found in error by the use of methods the sole merit of which is that they prevent risk-taking by excluding the presentation of ideas that may be refuted if they are erroneous. Because such ideas are usually stale trivialities, philosophers use techniques that mask the staleness and triviality of their presentations; usually these techniques are verbal: they employ logical or metaphysical terms. The difference between the two leading schools of philosophy today is in their choice between these two options: analysts employ logical terminologies, whereas phenomenologists prefer metaphysical terminologies; the simultaneous employment of the two vocabularies is known by foes as fence-sitting, muddles, or mix-ups and by friends as syntheses, mediations, or displays of broad outlooks.

It is, of course, regrettable that the search for ways to avoid error leads to techniques for masking rather than revealing them. But, we sympathize: the demand for the impossible must lead to pretense, so it is better to dismount those proverbial high horses and reconcile with mere mortal fallibility. As skeptics, we suggest that the best way to do so is to join us in skepticism. We suggest the abolition of all norms that aim at error avoidance and replacement with humbler and more reasonable ones. Obviously, there are two extremes to avoid here: (1) the irresponsible conscious advocacy of erroneous theories and the all-too-common indifference to the truth; and (2) the demand to avoid error and the all-too-common pretense that one is free of error. The aims should be to meet more reasonable targets, to avoid repeating corrected past errors, to raise questions, to seek new and interesting solutions, to debate them critically within the limits prescribed by circumstances, and to render these circumstances as conducive as possible to all critical assessments of new solutions. In brief, we recommend the replacement of the pretense of being always in the right with responsible conduct. We elaborate on this in the next chapter.

3

Science

In the previous chapter, we discussed the criticism of skepticism as a view that blocks the endorsement of any view. We parried this attack by arguing that it rests on the false assumption that views are chosen by mere decisions, whereas beliefs are largely given. This objection meets with a standard protest: the concern is not with belief but rather with rational belief. The received assumption is that irrational belief is forbidden and rational belief is obligatory and that skepticism denies that some beliefs are rational. What belief is rational? They say, for example, that the belief in tomorrow's sunrise is rational. Even if this were true, we have to admit that we do not choose to believe that; rather, we believe it is the result of some highly complex psychological processes that take us back to our childhood. In our scientific culture, we do not believe as adults in what we believed in as children. How come? What are the processes that we undergo as we forge or rather modify our views of the world? Under what conditions does the belief arise that a given statement is true? These are the questions that we discuss in this chapter.

The questions are important and for the following three reasons:

1. Understanding the psychology of belief may help resolve disputes rationally.
2. Evolutionary considerations suggest that humans possess built-in biological mechanisms for the formation, maintenance, and modification of beliefs, mechanisms that are sufficiently efficient to permit the survival of sufficiently many societies that are sufficiently diverse. (Humans survive in India despite beliefs common in that country that prevent restricting the damage

that cows and monkeys cause; treating tigers the same way would more significantly threaten their survival.) An evolutionary theory about this brings about automata emulating natural adaptability in order to learn and adjust to hostile environments. For this, we need ecological theories about hostile environments and perhaps, eventually, psychological theories of belief formation. Moreover, because we already possess machines that learn, however poorly, we may ask: Can these machines improve their beliefs (by some criteria of improvement)? Do they have beliefs in the first place? What are they? Answering such questions may contribute to progress in bridging the gap between human consciousness and automated computation and help to develop interesting ideas about how far this gap may be bridged. If it is impossible to bridge the gap entirely, the study of these questions may help shed new light on the distinction between humans and computers.

3. A psychological theory of the change of belief may help efforts to escape some limitation on belief, facilitate research, and make a difference in everyday activities, mainly between dogmatic and flexible patterns of thought and conduct.

Centuries of experience suggest that preaching is useless at best because it can do no more than expose the disadvantages of dogmatism, which is rampant despite general familiarity. The recent theory of learning from experience is this: not all experience teaches but only those that happen during imprinting or when adrenaline flows excessively. This theory suggests that all animals are dogmatic and that learning by modification of imprinted information is unusual. This is so because dogmatism has a survival value, a virtue that we must acknowledge and see how it can be retained while dogmatism is eschewed. The chief advantages of dogmatism are that it is a mode of retention of possibly vital information and that following it ushers decisive action.[1] The question, then, is: What alternative means are

---

[1] Another hypothesis concerns the evolutionary aspect of the process of individual belief-formation. The most common misreading of Darwinian or neo-Darwinian evolutionary theory concerns the fittest individual. The fittest is not fit but fit enough to survive the competition for its eco-niche and to procreate. This does not prevent errors and, indeed, avoidable pre-pubertal mortality occurs in all species. (See

there for efficient retention and decisive action? The understanding of beliefs and how they operate may help develop new ideas about them, and training individuals accordingly will be the least costly and dangerous cure for dogmatism.

Under what conditions are *erroneous* beliefs acquired and sustained? Daniel Kahneman and Amos Tversky, to mention one famous example, described certain patterns of probability-assessment formation that are systematically and repeatedly erroneous. Following them is no law of nature because it is easy to learn to avoid them. We do not discuss such patterns here because our concern is with basic processes of the fixation of belief, especially processes that people generally judge as rational – by whatever criteria of rationality and whatever this rationality may be.

The default popular view about beliefs is this: right beliefs are justifiable; people should believe all and only what they find justifiable. This view suffers from three shortcomings:

Sharon Moalem and Jonathan Prince, *Survival of the Sickest: A Medical Maverick Discovers Why We Need Disease.*) Nevertheless, such avoidance does occur; therefore, learning, even if much too narrow, at times aids survival. Learning linked to survival options often occurs in significant situations, either by imprinting or in life-threatening situations, wherein the neurochemistry of strong emotion imprints on long-term memory. In humans, we call the outcome of this kind of learning obsession. Under Freud's influence, due to his faith in error avoidance, we misread all obsessions as neurotic (perhaps to the exclusion of taboos). There is an important truth in Freud's confusion: humans are able to correct their errors; when they fail to do so, we suspect some obstacles on their way to improvement, usually fear. In accord with this, he observed, the intellectual ability to rectify error together with the affective inability to do so comprise a symptom of neurosis. He suggested that, invariably, the fear is rooted in the excitement that associates the acquisition of behavior patterns as obsessive. We suggest that this needs reinforcement – specifically, the fear of ridicule. It is possible to mitigate this fear by improving social norms by raising public awareness of the impossibility of avoiding all error. Whenever possible, the application of skepticism is helpful for neuroses because neurotics do behave dogmatically, as Freud noted. This is not always easy, but when it is, the false view of rationality hinders it. We should try more avenues for experimentation in many simple modes of cure. Encouraging a neurotic to make small experiments that may possibly relieve fear is better than many received techniques. When this is impossible, it may be advisable to find out why and combat the cause of the blockage rather than attack the neurosis head on. Freud's view that analyzing a neurosis is the only way to cure it is empirically refuted, and too often the literature overlooks this. Freud eschewed symptomatic treatment; however, if the alleviation of psychological distress is to be brought under the umbrella of medicine, sometimes the medical treatment of symptoms is indicated, as in the cases of sunstroke and cholera, in which the symptoms, not the disease, are fatal.

1. It rests on the presupposition that people choose the objects of their beliefs, at least if they are intelligent or well educated or rational. But this runs contrary to the common observation that beliefs are given.
2. It rests on the presupposition that statements are justifiable, which is contrary to its well-known (skeptical) refutations.
3. It rests on the presupposition that such justification generates unanimity among rational people. This runs contrary to the plain observation that disagreement is ubiquitous, especially among intelligent, well-educated, rational people.

We call attention to the following. Our skepticism does not deprive us of the use of the concept of belief the way the learned literature uses it. Although greatly varied, this literature is regularly in agreement about one important observation regarding belief: the discovery of a refutation of a statement taken to be true is a surprise. The level of that surprise may increase with the level of commitment or having taken the belief for granted, even if unknowingly so, as well as with the importance ascribed to it. Hence, conscious belief in two contradictory statements is impossible.[2] Hence, as Quine observed, a declaration of a belief in a contradiction demands reinterpretation. For a most conspicuous example, consider the statement that Hegelians and Marxists advocate that certain contradictions are real. It is obviously false; we may interpret it as the obvious truth that conflict is ubiquitous. Similarly, answering a yes-or-no question with yes and no, one means under some conditions yes, some conditions no, so that a yes-and-no answer is equivalent to "it depends" or to pointing at an ambiguity in the question.

The Critique of Empiricism

Empiricist philosophers demand belief in all and only those statements that are rational in which to believe. They assert that statements meriting rational belief are those that are reliable, credible, or believable. They are statements that logic or experience supports – directly or

---

[2] In his book, *1984*, George Orwell describes ultimate torture as the forcing of people to believe contradictions. God knows exactly what he meant by this.

indirectly (namely, as corollaries from such statements). Empiricists deem unproblematic support from logic. Because they admit that observations are problematic, they limit the reliability or credibility of observation reports to direct perceptions, to observations that reflect directly perceived reality in order to ensure that they are infallible.[3] The rules for inference that are used to yield reliable or credible conclusions are those of logic, deductive or inductive. To deem deductive logic as unproblematic is insufficient, empiricists reluctantly admit, because they want an inductive logic that would permit the deduction of theories from observation reports. Remember that Hume refuted the claim that this is at all logically possible. Empiricists take it for granted that he was in error because science exists. Empiricists ignore the fallibility of science and admit that no one knows what the rules of inductive logic are, therefore seeking them fervently.

Their efforts are doomed to frustration, we say. We now return to the paradoxes of induction, not as refutations of empiricist epistemology but rather as refutations of the empiricist psychology, the empiricist theory concerning the formation and the fixation of beliefs, the view that rational people believe statements inductively deduced from direct observations.

The first paradox, we may recall, was Goodman's. Defining the word *grue* to mean that an object is grue if and only if it is green until 2100 and blue thereafter, the two statements, "all emeralds are green" and "all emeralds are grue," are equally empirically justified, although the first seems true and the second absurd.

We argued that Goodman's paradox refutes the empiricist epistemological view that statements are inductively justifiable; we now argue that it refutes the psychological empiricist view of belief. For all we know, all observed emeralds are green, so we do admit that. The inductive rules of procedure, whatever they may be, cannot determine a rational preference for the conclusion that all emeralds are green over the conclusion that they are grue. But, actually, we disbelieve the second conclusion. Empiricism allegedly explains the rational choice

---

3 Surprisingly, W. V. Quine declared singular observation reports certain. See his "A Comment on Agassi's Remarks," *Zeitschrift für allgemeine Wisencchaftstheorie*, 1988, 19:117–118.

of beliefs, but as for the expectation of green over grue, it obviously does not.

We use the same strategy for the other famous paradox of induction, Hempel's paradox, which is that the empiricist theory implies the possibility of raising the conviction that all ravens are black by exhibiting both black ravens and non-black non-ravens, such as white shoes. Hence, Hempel refuted the empiricist's psychological theory of rational belief.

We present additional refutations later. First, we should introduce the quantitative theory that replaces the instantiation theory of empirical support: the probability theory of rational beliefs.

The Probability Theory of Rational Beliefs

The probability theory of rational beliefs states that every theory is credible to some degree, a degree that the calculus of probability helps determine in light of the total available empirical evidence. Thus, changing the stock of empirical evidence can alter the probability of hypotheses, reducing the credibility of one and raising that of another. This theory seems to explain how scientific revolutions occur, that science may relinquish faith in phlogiston in favor of oxygen, faith in Newton's gravitational force in favor of Einstein's curved space. Thus, counter-examples undermine a hypothesis thereby reducing its probability, whereas consistent examples support it thereby raising its probability. (In truth, we often believe people reputed as experts even though most of us have hardly glanced at the evidence; however, for now, we will let this ride.)

The calculus of probability yields with ease the following theorem: evidence that undermines a theory reduces its probability to zero. Empiricists ignore this: they are interested not in probability but rather in the rescue of induction. The calculus of probability assigns to any two statements a number between zero and one: the probability of the one (the hypothesis) given the other (the evidence) is a given fraction. What is given and how it is given is not the business of the calculus. It does not allow the computation of the probability of one assertion given another if the status of the evidence as given is tampered with. Therefore, empiricists have little choice but to demand that we do not consider as evidence any statement except an observation report that we deem certain. Otherwise, the calculus of probability does not apply. Such observation reports do not exist, of course.

The probability theory of rational beliefs is refuted by the following simple argument of Popper. Consider the brief time (between 1915 and 1919) when Einstein's theory of gravity was already known but Newton's theory of gravity was not yet refuted. According to the probability theory of rational beliefs, because at that time a lot of evidence supported each theory and none undermined either, each had a high probability, credibility, or rational degree of belief – that is, higher than 50 percent. (A theory the probability of which is less than 50 percent is less probable than its negation.) Now, consider the probability of the view that one of the theories is true. According to the calculus of probability, it is the sum of their probabilities. Hence, it is more than 100 percent. This is absurd.

The probability theory of rational beliefs is also open to criticism that rests on Hempel's paradox. Allegedly, the probability theory solves it. The frequency of non-black non-ravens is much higher than that of black ravens. The support due to an improbable observation is higher than that due to a probable one. Therefore, the support of observing black ravens in the theory "all ravens are black" is much higher than that of observing non-black non-ravens. But this does not eliminate the paradox because it still allows for the intolerable idea that all evidence is relevant to any hypothesis. How much irrelevant evidence does it render relevant? How many white shoes support "all ravens are black" as much as one black raven? Obviously, this is somewhat amusing; the irrelevance of some evidence for some hypothesis is vital for so many reasons.

The probability theory of rational belief is also open to criticism that rests on Goodman's paradox (in regard to the theory, "all emeralds are grue"). The considerations are the same as those stated in the previous paragraph, except that the relief that the probability theory allegedly offers here is from the claim that the new alternative that Goodman conjured is very improbable. Again, we may ask: How much do we have to boost the empirical support of the new hypothesis to compensate for this defect? Also, because the disjunction between many alternative Goodman predicates has an ever-increasing probability, this alone suffices to cancel any relief that the solution from probability may conceivably offer.

To add insult to injury, not only do optical illusions refute, even silly conjurer's tricks do as well. Consider the theory, "Rabbits cannot jump out of empty hats." Conjurers produce observations that refute it. We simply disbelieve the observation, not the theory – for the best reasons available or for no reason at all, as you like it. (The enjoyment of conjurers' tricks rests on the titillating seeming credibility of what runs against our deepest convictions.) The reasons, as it happens, refute the probability theory of rational beliefs, all protest to the contrary notwithstanding, because this theory leaves no room for false observations. Sir Francis Bacon knew this: first, he limited the set of scientific observations to those attested to (but, to no avail, for the conjurers stand at the ready); and, second, said Bacon, the dilution of false observations will render them harmless. The scientific tradition soon limited the set of scientific observations to those that are repeatable. This renders scientifically irrelevant the justification of generalizations about unique observations from the start. Moreover, because conjurers' tricks are repeatable, they are scientific. Their explanation is in the same style as the explanation of optical illusions.

The obvious response to our criticism is to flout this explanation or any other reasonable theory that exposes fake evidence as likewise fake. But, then, this theory may unwittingly allow for arbitrary immunization of any theory to all criticism by simply allowing the view of all refutations as fake. As long as this option is even faintly permissible, it renders error avoidance impossible. If, however, there is a guarantee that the proscription of fake evidence is not open to this abuse, then this is a guarantee that all genuine evidence is true. Such a guarantee is a theory of evidence. Does this theory rest on evidence? And is this evidence genuine or fake? It is all too easy to marshal fake evidence to support it.

Indeed, our argument itself smacks of a Sophist conjurer's trickery, and perhaps it is. Should we proscribe it? On what grounds? If no grounds are available, then the theory will disallow this proscription, no matter how sane the proscription may be. If it has grounds, then the question reappears: Is that ground solid or are we victims of another (higher level?) conjurer's trick? This, then, is a first step in an infinite Hume-style regression. Of course, in daily life, people rightly ignore such deliberations because they do not seek a promise that they will be infallible. Rather, they only do their best to behave as intelligently as they can and then they hope for the best. However, it never occurs to them, not even in their wildest dreams, that they can avoid all error and all optical illusions. Even the Pope's infallibility, in which all Catholics must believe, is not purported to make him infallible except when he speaks *ex cathedra* (and then he is – or should be – careful not to make any refutable assertions). Why are everyday guarantees not enough for philosophy? Because philosophy has made a profound observation, that we prefer our own culture to all other cultures, and that we do so uncritically and often to our great loss. This observation leads to a salient question: Why prefer my culture to yours? But philosophy gave this question the wrong answer: because my culture is scientific and so it is infallible. Some philosophers or, rather, some anti-philosophers, especially Wittgenstein, tried to proscribe the question. But the profound observation does raise the question, and it is salient even though most people do not ask it – at least not in daily life – and most philosophers still cling to the wrong answer thereto. The observation was that our preference for our views of the world rests on the sheer accident of our birth. The question was: What is the rule for the choice of a better view? And the erroneous answer was: choose only the views that you can prove. But this is too stringent a demand. Suffice it to say that we agree to seek explanations of what we know and discuss them critically and try to improve them in light of the criticism that we manage to elicit. On the whole, we suggest a simple policy: try to demand as little as you can and see if it delivers the goods. When you are disappointed, you better ask: What else should we demand? How then can we strengthen our demands minimally? Remember, it is easy to demand the moon; it is wiser to demand only what is vital or come as close to it as we can. Tradition prefers the bigger demand to the smaller one, on the suggestion that it is safer. This suggestion is amply refuted. We have no criteria for all situations about which demand is the safest. And when the bigger demand delivers observed harm and only promised benefits, said Popper (*The Open Society and Its Enemies*), those who suffer the harm in question deserve the benefit of doubt.

The Minimum Unexpectedness Hypothesis on Beliefs

We finally turn now to our answer to the psychological question: Under what conditions does one believe that a certain statement is true?

To reiterate, it is generally agreed that a sense of surprise accompanies the shattering of a belief: the discovery of a refutation of a statement believed to be true is a surprise. Let us see whether we can make do with this minimal supposition. Of course, we would like to assume that people seek the truth, but this is excessive, especially because, regrettably, many people are willing to settle for much less. So let us take one psychological characteristic of the possession of a familiar truth: the absence of surprise at its reappearance. This is not all, especially because it is not sufficient to characterize the relentless search for the truth that is such a characteristic of science. Moreover, even without science, quite possibly life with no surprise is intolerably boring (we return to this issue in Chapter 6). Nevertheless, let us examine this idea to see how far it can take us.

To summarize, then, our tentative (and possibly refuted) hypothesis is this: the function of ordinary belief (to exclude momentarily religious belief and its like) is to reduce surprise. Rightly or not, people tend to believe in a given statement if it reduces the unexpectedness of the apparent world, if it makes us expect our experiences as we live them:

1. People assign probabilities to events in some vague sense of probability, where the probable is the expected or the unsurprising.

2. Surprise or unexpectedness or improbability of events is relative to given beliefs. Events surprise if they are experienced more frequently than extant beliefs warrant, especially if those beliefs rule them out.

3. When people consider a new idea, they also consider the rationale for its being proposed in the first place, and if that rationale depends on some events, then people also consider the question of whether these events are to be expected.[4]

---

[4] This idea is very strong. It explains how ancient myths that still have currency are threatened by the study of their origins. We do not pursue this line of inquiry although we find it both exciting and useful.

Let us expand on this a little further. The improbable is surprising. Let us assume, then, that in some loose sense, surprise and improbability increase or decrease together. And, to repeat, what we consider probable and not probable depends on the theories that we entertain. Thus, to take the easiest – although not the best – example, assuming a coin to be fair leads to an obvious expectation: flipped repeatedly, it will come up heads equally as often as tails – more or less, that is (because small deviations are repeated experiences). Great deviations from this or systematic results are surprising. A theory that the coin is biased in a way that fits the observed systematic deviation from the expected result alters the expectation and reduces the level of experienced surprise. To take an extreme example, the observation of a series of heads only leads to the suspicion that both sides of the flipped coin are heads.

To reiterate, people believe a new idea if it raises the expectation of given experiences that are otherwise surprising. For example, the surprise that certain events regularly occur is reduced by postulating (spuriously or seriously, as the case may be) regularities that govern them. Thus, the supposition that all ravens are black renders quite expected the unexpected observations and initially surprising observation that ravens are regularly black (because without the theory, all colors may be expected). It is the theory that alters probabilities – quite in accord with the calculus of probability – and with them, the theory alters surprise values: in this light, the observation of a non-black raven would surprise and the observation of black ravens would not.

Now, note the following:

1. This hypothesis presents a sufficient condition for belief but not a necessary one. We say that explaining surprising events tends to create a belief; however, some beliefs are obviously due to different factors, often also of quite different sorts.
2. Like the probability theory of rational beliefs, this hypothesis assigns some probabilities to events, and both theories state that an explanation of an unexpected event raises our tendency to endorse the explanation. However, contrary to the probability theory of rational beliefs, this hypothesis does not assign probabilities to explanations; rather, it refers only to probabilities

of events. As mentioned previously, the idea that evidence can raise probabilities of theories is a version of the theory of induction and, hence, a refuted one.

3. The hypothesis is easily extendable to explain increases and decreases of degrees of belief or, rather, degrees of confidence: lowering the estimated probabilities of observations raises the degree of belief in their explanations. This idea is attributed to Ronald Fisher, who said that a hypothesis is likely in light of given evidence to the extent that it raises the probability of that evidence. That is, the likelihood of a given hypothesis in light of some evidence is the probability of that evidence relative to the probability of that evidence without that hypothesis.[5] For example, the greater the number of observable ravens, the lower the prior probability that all of them will turn up black. Therefore, the more observed ravens turn out to be black and none turn out to be non-black, the higher the confidence in the theory that all ravens are black because it makes this observation much more probable. Nevertheless, to repeat, this degree of belief is not a probability measure. Moreover, any correlation remains at best qualitative, not quantitative. There is no way and no need to render it quantitative.

We now apply the hypothesis and resolve the empirical versions of the paradoxes of empiricism. We resolve them regarding only psychology, ignoring epistemology, because we do not demand infallibility of accepted belief.

Consider the question that Goodman's paradox raises: Why does the theory that emeralds are grue have no adherent although so many philosophers know about it? Following the minimum unexpectedness theory, the question can be answered as follows. The statement, "all emeralds are grue," is arbitrarily constructed; one cannot escape notice of its arbitrariness: the moment in time for an emerald to change and the change itself that it has to undergo to qualify as grue are intentionally determined quite arbitrarily. The record of arbitrary theories is not good. The theory, "all emeralds are grue," thus does

---

[5] $L(H, e) = p(e, H)/p(e)$, where L = likelihood, H = hypothesis, e = evidence, and p = probability.

not reduce unexpectedness but rather increases it via the implication that the strange event following from a theory invented arbitrarily will turn out to be true.

To illustrate the dependence of our incredulity toward arbitrariness, consider a case in which the date of conversion of the color of emeralds is not selected arbitrarily. Imagine the idea that all emeralds change color in time, so that all emeralds are green until they age, when they turn blue. Imagine further that we have concluded this idea from our theory of the molecular structure of solids. Imagine, finally, that it so happens that all emeralds we can lay our hands on just now are young. There is nothing paradoxical about these assumptions. (This would be intuitively more acceptable if we speak about one of the synthetic gems that have recently entered the market rather than about emeralds.) We would then find nothing paradoxical about the need to consider both hypotheses: that our emeralds will remain green and that they will become blue when they age according to certain specifications. Inductivists may take this up and say that our claim that some assumptions are not arbitrary is our admission that some theories are inductively supported. This is not so. First, the suppositions that we discuss may be false. Thus, suppose that as it happens, there are different kinds of emeralds, and our experience is limited to one kind. Or perhaps the process of gem pigmentation decay accelerates or decelerates during some later phase, due to some hitherto unobserved specific phenomena. Broadening our horizons will make us realize our mistake. Inductivists say that this is why we should not jump to conclusions. Thus, when an inductivist theory is refuted, its adherents are quick to turn it into a demand. The hypothesis that we discuss here is descriptive, be it true or false. As to the distinction it makes between the arbitrary and the non-arbitrary, again, inductivists contrast the arbitrary with the justified; this hypothesis takes any reason that people admit as good enough because it is descriptive. Specifically, and to repeat, the hypothesis takes any explanation to be good enough if and to the extent that it reduces surprise. This is psychology. The methodological parallel to it is the demand to explain repeatable observations. This chapter is psychological, not methodological. Inductivists are mistaken when they ignore this: even if psychology could substantiate methodology, the two would remain distinct.

Consider, then, the empirical psychological variant of Hempel's paradox. His instantiation theory of credibility made him declare all evidence relevant to any given hypothesis. Let us report our experience: people – including philosophers – deem most available evidence as irrelevant to any given hypothesis. Our empirical variant of the paradox takes care of this. The irrelevance of a randomly given observation to a given hypothesis is their logical independence of each other. Their conjunction is not surprising in the least: the one does not exclude the other. And, as long as it does not render the observation unexpected, there is surprise. As it happens, cases of non-black non-ravens are not considered unexpected.[6] Hence, white shoes do not convince us that all ravens are black.

Take note of this. Here, we are speaking of the psychological hypothesis of the change of beliefs and, by our tentative hypothesis, this change of beliefs is prompted by its ability to reduce surprise. If that reduction is achieved by a new explanation, then people find that explanation credible. Whether they then change their belief or suspend judgment for a while longer is a different matter altogether. They may be dogmatists who cannot change their mind and who postpone decision until they forget. It is only if they act that their action is explicable. So, we claim that the hypothesis is limited to changes of opinion; it asserts that change is prompted by surprise; it does not assert that all surprise causes change of opinion.

So how does this psychological hypothesis apply to scientific research? This is still a complex matter. Inductivists identify the psychological and methodological or epistemological theories of the change of belief and then they have to limit their discussion to rational belief (which renders their descriptive theory prescriptive, we remember), taking it for granted that any received scientific theory is credible. This runs contrary to the notorious truth that science has sufficient room for some conflicting theories, such as that of Newton and Einstein. To accommodate for that, inductivists do not view as rational the belief in any scientific theory but rather only in the received one. The question

---

[6] There is some ambiguity here: the contrast with the expected may be the unexpected, the counter-expected, or both. The story that in science discovery is often accidental means that it is unexpected. More precisely, it is counter-expected. This explains why it counts significantly. (This is true for cubism and atonality as well: they are often counter-perspective and counter-tonality.)

becomes, then: What makes a researcher believe or disbelieve the latest theory? This question rests on the assumption that when researchers declare a new idea scientific, they believe in it. This is contrary to much historical evidence that makes much sense: researchers may assume that a theory has sufficient merit to draw attention without consulting their intuition about how credible they find it. They often postpone deliberation as long as they seriously consider the theory and its merits, and they offer their initial assessments as recommendations to examine the new theories for their merit and for their ability to withstand severe tests.[7] Indeed, researchers proliferate all viable hypotheses they can think of simply for the sake of the process of elimination in the hope of creating points of departure that bring forth new and hitherto unimagined hypotheses.

Thus, although our hypothesis applies to dogmatists and researchers alike, it does not apply to scientific research for the simple reason that researchers do not trust their own intuition; indeed, most great discoveries surprised their discoverers.[8]

Researchers, then, are seldom concerned with the credibility of the ideas that they investigate. Still, given that people do find irrelevant to a given hypothesis most of the information that they know, researchers into the psychology of the change of belief might ask: Does our hypothesis imply that any observation alters the credibility of any theory, even if only to a very small degree? No. The observation of an unsurprising event invites no additional theory to render it unsurprising; therefore, by that hypothesis, it plays no role in the formation of a new belief because it says that an increase in the credibility of a given theory is due to its successful reduction of unexpectedness.

Yet, our hypothesis does explain, for example, the limits of the applicability of our variant of Hempel's paradox. The paradox does not apply if, instead of referring to common characteristics (e.g., not being a raven and not being black), the hypothesis in question refers

---

7 Commentators who view Popper's theory of corroboration as a theory of inductive support find it difficult to allow for his claim that a good theory has a high degree of corroboration even before it undergoes any test. The meaning of corroboration for Popper is acceptability, and acceptability is not credibility but rather good candidacy for (further) tests. It is possible to take two competing theories as candidates for tests – even simultaneously (in crucial experiments) – not as candidates for rational belief.

8 See J. Agassi, *Towards an Historiography of Science*, 1963, 1967.

to *un*common characteristics. Consider, for example, the theory, "All bodies that fall are heavy." One might be convinced that this theory is true by observing light things that do not fall, such as airborne balloons. Common things are both heavy and tend to fall to the ground. The characteristics, "a body that does not fall" and "not heavy," are uncommon; therefore, observations of light bodies that do not fall are unexpected. As a result, one may enlist them to convince any hypothetical individual who does not believe the theory that all bodies that fall are heavy. One may object to this example by asserting that being heavy is simply the disposition to fall, just as being light is simply the absence of this disposition. Consider another example,[9] the theory that "all the objects above the size of a molecule are colored" (where items ordinarily deemed transparent are also recognized as however subtly tinted). Contrary to our variant of Hempel's paradox, it is possible to convince someone that this theory is true by referring to submolecular objects (e.g., an electron): they have no color. Once again, both characteristics – "being below the size of a molecule" and "not being colored" – are uncommon, at least to direct experience; therefore, examples of things that are below the size of a molecule and not colored do convince that all objects above the size of a molecule are colorful.

We hardly need to say that we are not surprised by the failure of empiricist philosophers of science to make sense of what people find credible and what they refuse to believe. They seek epistemological grounds for the preference of theories and identify the view of a theory as credible with lending credence thereto. This is a dual error. First, such grounds do not exist because all statements are doubtful. To this, they respond by observing that belief is repeatedly observed as people do believe this or that theory, and some are more reasonable about it than others. Indeed, there is interesting psychological knowledge about beliefs. People do find theories more or less convincing, more or less credible. But, here is their second error, and it is traditional as well as modern: it conflates epistemology and psychology so, with the defeat of empiricist epistemology, empiricist psychology is defeated as well. Here, we discuss only the alteration of credence and what

---

[9] Here, we follow an important rule: when an example becomes problematic, it should be replaced; if it is hard to replace, then it is not a mere example. Consider the famous philosophical expression: "consider a rational being, for example, a human being."

people find more or less credible than before (namely, psychology). We do not trouble ourselves in this context about the question of the rationality or the validity of accepted or unaccepted beliefs. Indeed, our tentative hypothesis applies to magically and scientifically minded people, to open-minded people, and to dogmatists. We do admit that people have beliefs. And we declare that the strength of our hypothesis is that it not only explains the change of beliefs that even dogmatists undergo but also the trouble they have in their struggle to maintain their beliefs, in their effort to fend off criticism of their views, whether or not empirical. They usually do so by the use of ad hoc hypotheses, but that is simply because these are more readily available than testable hypotheses. And what is most amusing about dogmatists is that they do not like ad hoc hypotheses any more than their critics, but they often find it necessary to learn to live with them.

Again, the empiricist philosophers of science claim that irrational beliefs do not interest them, that they study rational belief. This renders their views prescriptive rather than descriptive, we remember. To this, they may respond with the assertion that they consider scientific theories credible, so that their theory is descriptive. To reiterate, it is then refuted by observations of the attitudes of researchers toward theories.

More on the Paradoxes of Empiricism

There remains the question, then: What are the processes that govern the endorsement of the hypotheses in which we believe? There are a few candidates here, and we present them in the order in which we examine them: the absence of ad hoc adjustments, simplicity, Occam's razor, predictability, and tradition. In addition to these topics, all sorts of combinations are possible, of course, which we presented in the previous chapter when discussing the refutation of the empiricist epistemology. We now refer to these criteria as factors that partake in the psychological process of changing beliefs.

Theories Adjusted Ad Hoc

Let us begin then with ad hoc adjustments of theories. To reiterate, when a researcher continuously modifies a theory after finding a counter-example to it, the modifications that come most easily are those that exclude the counter-examples from its domain of applicability. The modified theory then encompasses increasingly fewer events and in ad hoc moves. These repeated corrections produce a series of theories with increasing ad hoc modifications. Credence in them diminishes, but rules of induction make no sense of this; to the contrary, it forces us to see nothing wrong with these moves and even to commend them because the known observations still support the modified theory in its ad hoc modifications no less than before and even more so. Inductivism thus supports most theories that fit information in as ad hoc a manner as possible – namely, those theories the specific corollaries of which are all predicatively confirmed – so that the cases to which they apply are already examined and harbor no surprise. The famous philosophers at the turn of the twentieth century, Ernst Mach and Pierre Duhem, understood all theories to mean exactly this. Duhem stated that when a theory is applied to a new case, the domain of applicability of that theory is extended only after the venture is a success. Look back, never forward.

Our hypothesis explains the incredulity of ad hoc as follows. Usually, we do not believe in a theory that underwent too many ad hoc modifications because it involves the highly unexpected event that all exceptions to the initial theory have already been *accidentally* observed. The probability that this is so is very small. Thus, the theory that has been repeatedly modified ad hoc has not reduced the element of surprise.

Of course, dogmatists do believe in ad hoc theories – and not only dogmatists but also many adherents to Newton's theory decades after Einstein won the consensus. They have to endorse ad hoc corrections to their views, no matter how reluctantly. Even scientific theories often undergo ad hoc corrections. Our hypothesis explains this reluctance.[10] Some people are dogmatic, some are credulous: the former find it difficult to depart from some of their beliefs, paying for it with a picture of the world that is less orderly than that of the less

---

[10] Philosophers and sociologists of science often defend the technique of modifying theories ad hoc on the grounds that researchers repeatedly use it. They ignore the reluctance that goes with such conduct and the delight in the replacement of the patched-up hypotheses with fresh and elegant ones.

dogmatic; the latter fall for theories more easily than the less credulous so that they too may believe in the less credible theories. Nevertheless, according to our tentative hypothesis, the function of the endorsement of belief even for the dogmatists and the credulous is the same as for all of us: the reduction of surprise. Yet, to explain the conduct of the dogmatists and the credulous, we need additional factors. The dogmatist finds it difficult to depart from past beliefs; the credulous is eager to fall for new ones. This is not new: Sir Francis Bacon, father of the modern theories of rational belief, did not try to explain beliefs but rather to advocate the disbelief in every nonscientific idea on the assumption of the almost total absence of scientific theory in his day. He explained this absence as the outcome of the scarcity of rational beliefs and found it natural to explain this scarcity by assuming the prevalence of dogmatism and credulity. He viewed these qualities the way we imitate them here; therefore, our hypothesis is descriptive and partial. Is it refutable? We return to this question later. Let us say now, however, that come what may, we should not view it as a principle of induction because it is a tentative hypothesis that invites tests – and we wish to render it testable, of course.

We may first extend our tentative hypothesis to add another empirical suggestion to it: researchers who cling to any theory after it was modified ad hoc do so because they hope to show that the exceptions are not accidental, that they are not due to accidental observations. Thus, our hypothesis goes very well with the familiar and obvious observation that it is difficult to refute a well-tested unrefuted theory. Hence, as David Bohm observed, when reputed researchers suggest ad hoc modifications to their theories, their peers extend the courtesy of waiting to see if they can render them less ad hoc before they decide to ignore them.

Simplicity and Occam's Razor

The reluctance to cling to explanations after they were modified ad hoc is often viewed as the converse of the eagerness to believe in simple explanations. To reiterate, when several measurements of a function of two parameters appear more or less on a line, people who see the results tend to conclude that the function is linear. This does not follow from the observed *data* because an infinite number of functions fit them.

Our hypothesis explains the phenomenon as follows: the linear function is the least arbitrary.[11] Once we allow any function, we have too many candidates. Therefore, the assumption that by sheer luck we hit on the right one does not reduce but rather raises the level of unexpectedness.

A similar analysis applies to Occam's razor, which is the demand to eliminate unnecessary entities. Our psychological hypothesis is that people do not tend to believe in theories that they judge as multiplying entities needlessly. The vagueness of all this is deadly for methodology but not necessarily for psychology because, in many situations, we have fairly durable ideas about what is and is not necessary, and then we judge the unnecessary as arbitrary.

Our hypothesis explains this psychological phenomenon in the same way that we explained simplicity: keeping stubbornly to defunct entities is, at best, a mere guess, and the assumption that such guesses are a reliable source of information increases rather than reduces the level of unexpectedness of experiences.[12]

In the name of Occam's razor, all sorts of entities were eliminated that no one misses, but some thinkers have also used it in support of their demand to eliminate all matter (idealism), or all minds (materialism), or God (atheism). All these moves were subject to intense philosophical debate – perhaps they still are. This is due to the absence of a criterion and even for a feel for what is and is not necessary, or even what the necessity was of which Occam spoke. Let us add that a debate rages over the very question: Do researchers endorse ad hoc hypotheses? Popper stated that they should not; Thomas Kuhn, Paul Feyerabend, and Imre Lakatos stated, as they so often did, that it

[11] Popper discussed the common preference for linear functions as their high testability. We do not dissent from his refusal to discuss credibility. Here, however, we link the recognition of testability to the psychology of credibility.
[12] To repeat, new empirical corroborations of a new theory that conflict with received theories are the most powerful motives for the change of views, a fact that fits our tentative hypothesis well and conflicts with inductivism. Bacon's criterion for novelty of observation is its logical independence of received theory: the observation is not expected. By contrast, we speak of counter-expected observations as surprising. The new corroboration is highly improbable and therefore very surprising.

is a mistake to tell them not to. We consider this dispute misguided: researchers do not trust their beliefs but rather try out diverse options, just as detectives may examine evidence even when they are convinced that the suspect is not guilty or that the evidence is planted. Finally, one can always let the beard grow for a while longer to see how it feels and only then consider shaving it.

Predictions and Explanations

Let us now turn to the difference between predictions and explanations. To reiterate, contrary to the standard version of empiricism, predictions that come true are more convincing than explanations of known events.

Our tentative hypothesis explains why. It is usually easier to create a new theory that successfully explains given events by offering generalizations than to predict new events correctly. Therefore, the event of devising a theory that provides a new true prediction is more unexpected than devising a theory that provides a new explanation of past events. Consider an explanatory theory that also provides testable predictions that turn out to be true. We do not expect a conjecture to be successful in predicting unexpected events. Hence, when a theory successfully predicts them, the assumption that the theory is true drastically reduces the level of unexpectedness.

Our tentative hypothesis explains more: when a researcher comes up with a surprisingly strong theory, we may examine its structure and see if its strength is due to some verbal trick or if it expresses some new intelligent idea or remarkable corollary; the credibility of the theory increases even before any prediction. This is important for cases in which predictions are difficult to come by: it takes some convincing to persuade a researcher to prepare a new experiment.[13]

Also, in the unusual case in which two equally explanatory theories compete, we do demand them to compete by predictions to break the tie between them. This is a crucial experiment that makes no sense

---

[13] This was first noted by Popper, as his theory explains it: the degree of testability of a new theory can be high or low even before any test. This is important because even if there are not too many new ideas to test, preparing a test takes great effort.

to empiricists, all protests to the contrary notwithstanding.[14] Popper proved impossible the traditional empiricist theory that deems rational belief as abiding by the calculus of probability. He suggested that if one insists on rational belief, one should consider the failure to refute a theory a better measure. For our part, we carefully avoid recommendations. We assert that often researchers do follow his suggestion and as an instance of the more general case of the reduction of unexpectedness.

Thus, we explain the change of mind that researchers may experience as a group after certain spectacular and crucial experiments. This psychological phenomenon we explain by our psychological hypothesis that is more general because the psychology of researchers is not general, and even researchers do not all follow scientific criteria except in research. They then often rely on tradition.

Thus, the situation is rather unexpected. Popper's critics are in error because they habitually and traditionally confuse psychology with methodology. Popper claimed that significant research is explicable as results of the application of his methodology. We add to this the observation that the psychology of research appears distinct from methodology, and we have managed to bring them closer together than Popper noted even though we used the psychology that runs parallel or analogous to his methodology. But, to repeat, we do not wish to run this parallel or analogy too closely: psychology does differ from methodology, and then our parallel or analogy breaks down. To see that, we continue with our examination of the criterion that conflicts with this parallel or analogy: the use of tradition as a criterion for credibility. This too is not what we recommend: we recommend no belief, least of all in research.

Tradition

Tradition influences belief. This is a repeated, unrefuted observation. It is very much the expected situation. Normal education conveys traditional theories, leading to the expectation that they are true. Therefore, when certain observations are explained by two competing

---

[14] Unlike many of his followers, Bacon approved of crucial experiments; however, in this (as in many other things) he was inconsistent.

theories, only one of which is traditional, the tendency is to endorse the traditional one a priori.[15]

Our tentative hypothesis, you may recall, is partial. It presents a sufficient condition for the endorsement of a belief, not a necessary one. This applies also to the role of tradition. Our tentative hypothesis does not refer to the difference between slow and fast learners. It also does not consider the prevalence of differences of opinion within the same community despite its members sharing the same fund of knowledge and more or less the same tradition. Moreover, some people do not find it possible to deviate from tradition and they may even be unable to envisage such a deviation. These phenomena are very interesting; they seek a psychological explanation, and we recommend trying to develop one. We do not do so here, however, because it is beyond the scope of this study.

Is our psychological hypothesis testable, then? Following what we said previously, one way to refute it is to find a case in which certain repeatable observations are explained by two competing theories, one of which is more in line with tradition than the other and, contrary to our hypothesis, the endorsed explanation is the non-traditional. This, however, is questionable because we can explain the anti-traditional preference as the eagerness to endorse radical tendencies, and we may explain these and other tendencies by different ideas. Still, this additional explanation may be testable and thus restore the testability of our initial hypothesis. This is the norm in the social sciences, where liberty with added parameters is open to further discussion on the condition or in the hope of success in rendering an untestable hypothesis testable.

Hence, all we can say now is that our hypothesis allows for tradition to play a role. This is not much, but it is more than empiricism allows because it rejects all traditions except the scientific tradition and it does so on the (erroneous) understanding that the scientific tradition is utterly radical – namely, that the scientific tradition is free of all views except the ones that are proven.

---

[15] A priori means before. In philosophy, the term *a priori* stands for *a priori knowledge* – knowledge that does not depend on experience – as contrasted with *a posteriori*, which stands for *a posteriori knowledge* meaning knowledge that depends on experience. Not so in other kinds of texts, such as legal or scientific texts. As skeptics, we have no use for the philosophical term.

Applications

We turn now to practical applications of our hypothesis, as follows:

1. One obvious application refers to a practical way for convincing
    people, which is not very appealing but which in some cases is
    necessary, such as the search for a partner in business or matri-
    mony or political exchanges of all sorts. For, in any case, to con-
    vince is to influence the endorsement of ideas, whether concern-
    ing the suitability of prospective partners or the practicality of
    a political program. Indeed, we contend, efforts to create con-
    viction in a certain idea lead to listing conceivable events for
    the idea in question to explain and to evaluating the degree of
    unexpectedness of each of them. Realizing this improves per-
    formance.

2. This hypothesis is also applicable to software programs that issue
    classifications or predictions for new cases (e.g., computerized
    diagnosis).[16] Some of these programs issue the classification
    by applying rules: a certain syndrome renders likely a certain
    diagnosis. Now, during a medical examination, we may face a
    situation in which different rules lead to different diagnoses and
    prognoses (predictions of sorts) in regard to the case under clas-
    sification. Following our hypothesis, emulating human psychol-
    ogy, such cases can find their resolution by calculating which
    prediction implies fewer unexpected events, although the exact
    method is beyond the scope of the current work.[17]

3. When building a model to explain given data, we should check
    the model's ability to reduce the level of unexpectedness of
    events – namely, its ability to explain. This is not news. Also,
    a model that does not reduce the level of unexpectedness,
    because it entails no prediction, is no better than any alternative
    model. We naturally tend to endorse what seems to us closer to
    common sense. This is how tradition comes into play unless we

---

[16] Nathaniel Laor and Joseph Agassi, *Diagnosis: Philosophical and Medical Perspectives*,
1990, Ch. 3.

[17] A software program that applies this method, WizWhy, can be downloaded from
www.wizsoft.com. See also Abraham Meidan and Boris Levin, "Choosing from Competing Theories in Computerised Learning," *Mind and Machines*, 2002, 12.

are critically minded. But different traditions offer entirely different ideas as to just what common sense is, even in regard to the place of sheer coincidence and outright notions of magic.

4. Pursuant to building explanatory models, when seeking an explanation, we should consider the possibility of a fluke. Darwinian evolutionism can serve as an example: prior to Darwin, leading naturalists considered the variety of species inexplicable or explicable, if at all, as expressions of divine intervention (which amounts to the same). The Darwinian theory (as well as the neo-Darwinian theory) offers a pattern of explanations as processes of accidental changes, only the fit of which survive long enough to breed. Following this pattern, we may hope to render explicable a greater part of the variety of observed species. So, the theory reduces at once the level of unexpectedness of this variety. Note that, as a scheme, Darwinism is hardly refutable. Still, many of us endorse it because it reduces the level of unexpectedness and squares biology with the naturalist view of the world that is at the base of the scientific venture, at least better than its earlier competitors.

5. Finally, our hypothesis explains the generally expressed complaint that the social sciences are trivial. Many of the observations that the theories in the social sciences explain are expected; as a result, these theories look trivial. There are exceptions, of course, but those who complain do so under the overall impression that most theories of the social sciences fail to reveal unexpected discoveries. The practical instruction is, therefore, as follows: look for unexpected general observations, try to create a theory that explains them, and then try to test it by reference to still fewer expected observations.

The last point is, of course, an echo of Popper's theory of scientific method. He excluded psychology, especially any psychological hypothesis regarding the change of beliefs. Without failing to admire Popper's tenacity, we reintroduced a psychological hypothesis regarding changes of beliefs – as a separate hypothesis to be tested and improved upon. Now, assuming that our hypothesis is true, do we like it? Do we wish our beliefs to behave as it describes? If not, what can we do about it? Moreover, can we change and improve the psychological mechanism of our beliefs? These are good questions, and we can offer only outlines of answers. We assume that no rational person willingly desires to believe falsehoods. And so, it is worthwhile to study the question: What is the mechanism for self-deception? Also, we assume that repeatable refutations impose the relinquishing of the refuted views. Inasmuch as we can control our psychology, we may then train ourselves to open up to all the alternatives that we can find, and do so critically. This is easier said than done: it often takes more courage than is readily available.

4

Ethics

Skepticism in Ethics

In the previous chapters, we presented skeptical epistemology. In this chapter, we present skeptical ethics.

We follow the same approach adopted in the previous chapters. We start by endorsing skepticism, according to which there is no moral knowledge and no final justification of any moral judgment. While refusing to reduce ethics to psychology, we present a tentative psychological theory regarding the conditions under which a mode of conduct is considered moral in order to place it on the agenda for public discussion.

Philosophers concerned with ethics have traditionally studied the following questions:

1. What renders a moral judgment valid moral knowledge – namely, certain or at least plausible?
2. What should we do to acquire new valid moral judgments?

We endorse the skeptical answers to these questions, which are as follows:

1. No moral judgment is certain or plausible; there is no moral knowledge; no moral judgment can be fully justified. (Again, conditional justifications are available, but they beg the question of validity of the outcome.)
2. No method can fully guarantee the validity of any moral judgment. (Again, conditional guarantees are available, and most of them are poor.)

Skepticism was always unpopular – in epistemology and ethics alike.

The arguments against skepticism in ethics run parallel to those against skepticism in epistemology that we reviewed in previous chapters. The argument in ethics is that moral skepticism is absurd because it implies the following unacceptable conclusions:

1. There are no moral rules; nihilism is true and valid.
2. Rational settlement of moral disagreements is impossible.
3. Punishment is immoral.

We now consider these assertions and show that they are not corollaries of skepticism, thereby diffusing traditional objections.

Two semantic remarks: First, convention suggests that "ethics" and "morals" (or "morality") be distinguished, ethics being the criteria for the morals that are rules for morality – namely, proper conduct. This distinction is not always rigorously maintained. We do not make much use of it. In particular, when discussing criteria for proper conduct rather than proper conduct itself, we say so explicitly. Second, convention suggests that we may speak of the truth of statements only if they constitute descriptions, not judgments (e.g., rules, prescriptions, recommendations, and evaluations). Instead of speaking of judgments as true or untrue, philosophers usually prefer to speak of them as valid or invalid, as the case may be. Yet, here we face an ambiguity to which as skeptics we are rather sensitive: the claim that a descriptive statement is valid is often taken as the claim that it is justified. Now, although we say that descriptions are never justifiable, we nevertheless think that they are sometimes true; in parallel to this, although we say that prescriptions are never justifiable, we do think that they are sometimes true or proper or right – valid in the sense also often received within current philosophy. So we choose to be strict here and speak of the truth or falsity of descriptions and of rightness and wrongness of prescriptions.

We return to the objections to moral skepticism. The first of these objections is the claim that moral skepticism implies nihilism. This objection rests on the following false claim: if no moral judgment is certain or plausible, then no moral judgment is right. To say that the rejection of certitude in morality is nihilistic is merely to state this false claim differently. This is confusion (or the identification) of rightness with certainty; it leads to the denial of the existence of doubtful truths and rights. On the contrary, skepticism includes the following claims:[1]

1. No moral judgment is certain or plausible.

Nevertheless,

2. Some moral judgments are right, valid, correct, happy, and so forth.

To see that an uncertain moral judgment can be right, consider genuine moral disagreement among serious reasonable individuals,[2] such as one concerning lying to prevent murder or stealing food to feed the hungry. In such cases, the disagreement may be rational. Therefore, each of the conflicting possible judgments is reasonable and uncertain; yet, because the dissenting parties reject each other's view, they cannot both be right.

The second of these objections to skepticism in ethics rests on the view that it blocks all rational resolutions of moral disagreements or disputes. The skeptical answer to this is the same as the answer to the parallel objection in epistemology: the objection rests on the assumption that moral judgments are freely chosen.[3] They are not. Our moral judgments are given; they are the result of psychological processes. This raises the question: What are these psychological processes and how much can they be influenced by rational means? We address this question shortly.

[1] These claims are not quite alternative answers to the questions posed herein. The logic of questions and answers calls a pseudo-answer the response to a question that is the denial of the supposition on which it rests. Thus, all skeptical responses to questions that are searches for blanket justifications are pseudo-answers.

[2] Harry Lustig, "Physics in Theater," *Forum on Physics & Society of The American Physical Society*, 35, January 2006, responds interestingly to the remark of the nineteenth-century German playwright, Friedrich Hebbel: "In a good play, everyone is right" *apropos* of the tremendous moral problems that the intriguing play *Copenhagen* (which portrays the meeting during World War II between Niels Bohr and Werner Heisenberg) rudely overlooks. By right, that playwright did not mean morally correct but rather morally reasonable. And, in the play in question, they are all reasonable even though in truth and by any reasonable standard, Heisenberg was not.

[3] To the extent that moral disputes represent diverse interests, people often reach practical settlements by compromise, and compromise certainly falls outside this discussion because its choice is always ad hoc. Our present discussion concerns theoretical disputes, which are often hypothetical; therefore, again, they need not reflect the axioms to which the participants in it are committed.

The third objection to skepticism is that it leads to the absurd conclusion that all punishment is – if not immoral – then amoral. If no moral judgment is justified, then there is no justification for the enforcement of any moral judgment by any means, including the means of punishing those who violate morality. In such a case, what we deem the crime is morally no different than what we deem the punishment. That this conclusion is unacceptable to many is no objection to moral skepticism. The situation is fully analogous to what we met when we discussed a similar objection to epistemological skepticism. Both rest on the false assumption that rationality requires final justification. A specific punishment may be moral according to one system of ethics or one moral standard or set of criteria but not according to another.[4] Fortunately, all humans come to increasingly share the same morality. In part, this is possibly due to some common inherited factors, which may indeed be judged psychological.[5] Whether this is so we can leave to another discussion: we lack both a general theory and sufficiently wide-ranging data for a proper global comparative ethics.

We have no wish to justify ethics or morality because we find it always better to improve than to justify. And, indeed, the main burden of any system of ethics that is worth the effort is to render moral improvements possible and even to facilitate such improvements, propose the outline of some new improvements, and pave the way to their implementation.

---

[4] Karl Popper's monumental *The Open Society and Its Enemies* presents two kinds of ethics – collectivist and individualist – assuming that, historically, collectivism came first. This is a very significant and profound idea. It strangely and surprisingly does not impinge on our more radical idea that the two converge. For, inasmuch as individualists concede that the collective interest is worth defending, they do so on the understanding that guarding the collective is in the individual's interest – and *vice versa*. The dispute between the two parties can come to the fore only in situations of conflict between them – which, alas, is all too common, as when a commander orders a soldier to go on patrol. Here, both collectivist and individualist use the same military criteria to judge whether the command was right. These criteria are much more considerate in democracies than in dictatorships, however. Yet, even in tyrannies, we propose, disputes can and should be resolved as amicably as possible. We may still be in dissent from Popper here because we consider disputes between individualists and collectivists resolvable and at times resolved, and perhaps he did not. We do not know.

[5] As Popper observed (*op. cit.*, Chap. 24, Sec. iii), the psychological aspect of the situation is that of sympathy to the suffering of other people, and the moral aspect of it is the demand to take heed of it and try to reduce it.

Toward a Psychological Theory of Moral Judgments

One of the main objections to skepticism in ethics that we have
encountered rests on the view that it blocks the rational resolution
of moral disputes. The skeptical answer to this, we say, is parallel to
the parallel objection in epistemology: it rests on the false assumption
that moral judgments are chosen although they result largely from
some given psychological factors. This raises the questions that we
now consider: What are these psychological factors and what exactly
is their contribution? What of the contribution is to the good and
what should we do to enhance and weaken, respectively, the desirable
and undesirable influences of our psychology? Let us begin with the
psychological question: Under what conditions does one endorse a
given (right or wrong) moral judgment?

This is an ontological question that few psychologists and no
philosophers have studied. Philosophers are concerned with the justification of moral judgments; traditionally, they came up with only two
options: the ethics of intentions and the ethics of consequences. It is
clear that, as the famous saying goes, the road to Hell is paved with
good intentions. Nevertheless, consequences are seldom due to mere
deliberation, moral or otherwise. As we noted previously, conduct is
questioned if it has led to disasters despite the good intentions that
presumably stand behind it and usually while questioning the degree
of responsibility of the actors who are officially responsible. We take
note at this juncture that ethics should concern itself less with moral
motives and more with moral inhibition: it was the loss of moral inhibition that led to the worst disasters in human history in the twentieth
century. And, because the concern of traditional studies of ethics is
concerned with justification, the studies are understandably lacking.
We take it that here skepticism can make an important contribution
by merely drawing the attention of students of ethics and morality to
this serious lacuna in their studies (even if they reject our diagnosis of
it as rooted in the desire to justify).

Developmental psychologists, especially Piaget and Kohlberg, studied this question ontogenetically (i.e., relating to the growth of a child)
without discussing it phylogenetically (i.e., relating to the growth of
the species): they reported that the morality of children develops in
stages. Let us ignore here the valid criticism of their reports as grossly
biased (i.e., in favor of males in modern society) and notice just one

important development that they reported as it reflected their moral views. At first, they claimed, children learn to obey rules just to avoid punishment; later, they do so to meet other people's expectations; and only still later do they realize that there are universal moral principles that are better obeyed. Thus, clearly, these observations rest on the assumption that adults know that some principles are right. As skeptics, we assert that some people – not all of them (particularly not the relativists) – assume that this is so, and regrettably too few of them are willing to subject their assumptions to criticism.

As Freud's theories are no longer upheld even by the psychoanalytic association we need not criticize it; yet we should remember what his aim was. He intended his theory to explain moral development ontogenetically and phylogenetically alike. To resolve the oedipal conflict, he said, children identify with their fathers and thereby adopt their moral norms. The very existence of conflict, he rightly observed, is the source of all morality. (In the absence thereof, we may act spontaneously with no need for moral considerations.) Yet, his view that all initial conflicts are the same is false. Taken as empirical, it does not hold for societies with family structures that Freud could not envisage (Bronislaw Malinowski); otherwise, it is inborn and not due to experience (Jacques Lacan).

Students of evolution deal with a different aspect of the question: they ignore the origins of any mode of conduct and the question of whether they are right or wrong because they wish to explain the survival of any mode of conduct (of humans as well as lower animals) that has survived as its positive contribution to the survival of that species once it appeared and won popularity. This is explaining the survival of a mode of conduct as preferred by natural selection. As ethological studies (i.e., studies of animal behavior, especially as it occurs in natural environments) turn to morality, then, they become searches for Darwinian models that explain how certain given moral norms have survived by being reinforced by natural selection. Presumably, the models present given norms as having survived because the societies that sustain them survive and the ability of these societies to survive as due (at least, in part) to the contribution of these norms. This last assumption is highly questionable: traits that impede prospects of survival are known to have survived because, evidently, they do not impede them too much. Thus, many received codes also are clearly immoral and harmful but not to destruction. Perhaps some tribes have venerated tigers, as the Hindus venerate cows, but were devoured by tigers. We do not know, but we do know that some societies are extinct despite their high morals and some survive despite their faith in certain atrocities.

Our interest here is in a different aspect of the matter. We wish to explain neither the origins of moral codes nor their survival, much less their survival value – namely, their contributions to the survival of the species or groups that practice them. Rather, we seek the psychological processes that accompany extant moral judgments, be they right or wrong – the psychological processes that to some measure are possibly responsible for these judgments: Under what conditions do people endorse a given moral judgment?[6]

As our tentative answer to this question, we suggest the following general psychological theory:

1. People tend to sympathize with the suffering of others and to consider immoral any act that increases suffering (Hume's principle).

Such acts may be necessary; they are well known as necessary evils. Now, committing a necessary evil may be excusable, and even imperative, but it still is evil, which is our point.

2. People are normally ready to consider (as best they can) which rules they might legislate if they were rulers of the world aiming at maximization of the welfare of humanity as a whole.

This second assumption is hypothetical. One might think that it is therefore not amenable to any empirical considerations. We hope that it is because it refers to people's dispositions, which – as many researches have illustrated – may at times be easily open to empirical investigations.[7]

---

[6] We dodge here the important question of the contribution of the endorsement of a norm to practice and discuss only norms, not practices. We touch on these later, nevertheless, but only as part of the critical examination of our views.

[7] Let us mention one recent factual study of ethics, led by Michael Koenigs and Liane Young, because such studies are still very rare: "Damage to the prefrontal cortex increases utilitarian moral judgments," *Nature*, published online on March 21, 2007. It has caused quite a stir. It offers evidence to the hypothesis that there are two somewhat independent areas in the brain – in charge of utilitarian thinking and sympathy, respectively. The authors pursue a line of thought akin to the one we propose here, which invites further similar studies.

Maximizing the Welfare of Humanity

What is the proper way to measure the welfare of humanity as a whole? This is a difficult question with which many students of ethics have dealt, as well as many economists, sociologists, and politicologists. It is too difficult; therefore, we can seek out easier versions thereof or strive to break down the question into smaller questions. Consider, then, the partial question for a given specific move: Can we judge whether it will increase or decrease the welfare of humanity as a whole? This question is easier but still too difficult. We may assume that we can judge with ease whether any given move will increase or decrease the welfare of any single individual. (This is questionable, too, but we will let this ride.) We may then ignore as unproblematic also the cases in which the welfare of one individual increases with no decrease of the welfare of any other individual, or vice versa, and concentrate instead on conflict situations, in which one event increases the welfare of one individual and decreases the welfare of another. Is there a rule that would determine for us which of these cases is morally commendable and which is morally reprehensible? Unfortunately, researchers are stuck even with this very preliminary question; they cannot even release the unproblematic cases because they seek justifiable rules that explain their unproblematic character. This may be reasonable, but then they also want the rules to do so with finality. Researchers naturally have to cover normal situations of this sort first: unreasonable assumptions lead them to futile search.

Some cases of conflict are unproblematic. Normally, we all deem theft clearly reprehensible and charity clearly commendable. This is not enough of a guide in such matters, however, because there are exceptions to this judgment; anyway, as long as we cannot explain it, we should not relax our search. As for exceptions, common sense tells us that it is right to take just a little money from the very rich to save a child starving under our eyes. Most researchers seek rules of this kind that are comprehensive. This drives them to the search for the ultimate rule that provides sound criteria for deciding how far the welfare state can and should go in this direction and what would be going too far; they want the rule to do all this and more, and with finality. We see here, incidentally, how close the search for finality is to the hope to do away with all debates, including rational debates and democratic parliamentary debates – and, thus, with democracy as such.[8] In what follows, we present different conflict situations that, we argue, are easy to judge as better eliminated. But these pertain to legislation, whereas the literature we have thus far discussed altogether ignores legislation. For this, we have to say a word on the welfare state because on this, paradoxically perhaps, the literature proliferates.

We consider it obvious that with all the possible merit of considerations of welfare and the welfare state, as long as they do not seem clearly relevant to the psychological theory that we advocate here, we should postpone comments as long as possible. For the time being, we speak of one possible way to improve human welfare and in the abstract rather than in diverse concrete cases. We return to this point and endeavor to cover wider considerations later.

A semantic note: We use the word *welfare* rather than the word *utility*. Although the latter is more frequent in the studies of ethics and welfare economics, we find it too technical and pretentious, as can be seen from the inadequacy of its translations into some foreign languages. We use *welfare* in its common, rather vague, sense because this serves us well enough in this initial stage of discussion (without objection to replacement of the vague concept with the precise one used in the economic literature, even though we think that there are other, more adequate ways to render it precise).

Let us then discuss the patterns of rules that, according to our tentative psychological theory, people are willing to legislate as means for the maximization of the welfare of humanity.

The minimal requirement is that such legislation should aim at the prevention of situations in which a rational selfish action lowers the welfare of humanity.

Some situations are usually presented by way of the example or set of examples known as "the prisoners' dilemma," and we make do with discussing those. The example is the outcome of the following observations. Everyone knows how to make decisions when they affect no one

---

[8] The idea that the demand for certitude in political theory leads one away from democracy is the thesis of the celebrated book by Jacob Talmon, *The Origins of Totalitarian Democracy* (1951). See also John Watkins's brilliant "Epistemology and Politics," *Proceedings of the Aristotelian Society*, 1957–1958, 58:79–102; reprinted in J. Agassi and I. C. Jarvie, *Rationality: The Critical View*, 1987, 151–167.

but oneself. (This is not true or else psychotherapy would be unnecessary, but because it is a prevalent supposition, let us allow it here.) It is also easy to make decisions in concert because this is the heart of the democratic process. (This is also not true or else we would have no crises in democracies and no tyrannies, but let us allow this here too.) What remains is the case of two individuals whose decisions affect each other but who cannot act in concert. For our discussion, let us make them two criminals in different cells so that they cannot communicate. (They are ordinary citizens in ordinary situations, really; we allow this story because it is standard and it is a mere flourish anyway.) We want their interests to be in concert. Let us assume that there is questionable evidence against them; therefore, it is in their common interest to be faithful to each other and keep their mouth shut. The story then must have a happy ending. So let us bring in the authorities to alter the situation in the hope of making each betray the other by making the possible outcome of their conduct depend on their surmise of each other's conduct. The authorities make rules, then, as follows. (The rules, as is the whole story, are idealizations of common circumstances: they render a vague situation more distinct.) If one prisoner keeps silent and the other becomes a state witness, the silent partner is severely punished and the state witness walks. If both talk, then they may expect a somewhat reduced sentence. If both are silent, however, they both suffer light punishment. Assuming (as usual in the literature in question) that both act rationally in accord with their self-interest, then it is obvious that if they trust and care for each other, they should both keep silent. Many dramas rest on the tension that the demand for trust raises. In these dramas, the prisoners elicit our sympathy, so they are seldom criminals – they are often made into spies or captive soldiers. The tension increases as the captors test the mutual trust by raising stakes. One prisoner may suggest intent to betray, yet the other must know that this is deception and that trust must prevail. When trust does prevail, the result is that, in the end, they both walk out of a tight trap with a slight punishment at most. Other dramas rest on trust and betrayal, showing that trust was misplaced. The present deliberation is not concerned with the rights and wrongs of trust or distrust; we take these as given. So, we conclude, with not much trust or caring between the two prisoners, that both should decide to talk because this decision will make each better off independent of the other's decision.

The prisoners' dilemma, to repeat, is an exaggerated distinct model for real-world moral conflicts with interdependent decisions, as the following considerations illustrate. Consider a world with no punitive measures and no conscience. Consider theft on the (realistic) supposition that stolen goods depreciate in value. For every individual taken separately, then, theft is advantageous, yet for the public, it is not. Hence, this is a version of the prisoners'-dilemma situation. Thus, it is reasonable to legislate for effective severe punitive measures and instill strict moral consciousness so as to render theft scarce. This is an example of the theory we tentatively advocate here as the psychological root of morality.

To generalize this and bring it closer to reality, let us take for granted that, to some extent, we are all both rational and selfish. A legislator who wishes to take care of the welfare of humanity at large should therefore try to prevent situations that give rise to prisoners'- dilemma situations – as much as is reasonably possible, of course. The best known means to this end are punishment, social pressures, indoctrination, and education[9] because we wish to reduce the attraction of whatever one can achieve by the means of selfish conduct in prisoners'-dilemma situations in a manner that we deem injurious to human welfare in general. And it is realistic to suppose that punishment, the sense of shame, a guilty conscience, and humiliation – or, alternatively, moral autonomy – are the means for achieving this goal. In other words, we should make prisoners' conditions such that the option of mutual betrayal would be reasonably unattractive.

Almost all countries legislate and implement such measures. Why, then, is theft not very rare? Why are so many of us thieves? These are difficult questions because we do not know how to assess the tolerable level of theft. The standard view is that when theft is so prevalent that it begins to threaten the economy or the legal system, then people in charge of the situation – legislators, bureaucrats, or educators – make some effort to reduce the level of theft. For example, self-service stores depend on a low level of shoplifting: when it exceeds a given level, it

---

[9] As long as corporation representatives could bribe foreign dignitaries with impunity, authorities could not stop them. Legislation of punitive measures did.

renders self-service stores less economical than those with attendants. In some countries, stores tolerate shoplifting; in other countries, they cannot afford to: the people in charge of self-service stores must seek new means to curb shoplifting (e.g., the employment of detectives or conspicuous surveillance cameras) as long as it is cheaper than the employment of store attendants and security guards.

This consideration is fairly simple. Different cases of theft are much more problematic, for example, than those related to drug abuse (and most petty thefts in the modern world are). So let us ask instead: How many decide to be professional thieves, and what is the level of incidental theft? And what determines these two kinds of socially harmful activity?

Obviously, existing penalties are insufficient deterrents: thieves dismiss the common views about the risk of penalty. They care little about the social stigma of shame or guilt, do not mind overmuch the hardship of short periods in jail, and consider the risk of punitive measures a fair bet. Theft undertaken by ordinary citizens is less frequent because the penalty they may suffer is higher because they shun stigma; the risk they undertake is thus considerably higher, particularly because they are inexpert and the risk includes the loss of a job. (This is well illustrated in the familiar process in which the state machinery turns young offenders into hardened criminals.)

This leads to a practical suggestion.[10] Rather than increase punishment, it is better to make use of the very difference between the social environments of criminals and law-abiding citizens. Obviously, in their own subsocieties or social environments, criminals are not deviants. Assume that criminals live in subcommunities that do not respect the law, so that they meet no social pressure to behave morally. Assume also that they can receive help to join some more law-abiding subcommunities. We can then reduce crime levels by helping enough

[10] The vast literature on criminal sociology, in particular on the causes of criminal behavior, aims at practical suggestions rather than at explaining crime. In particular, the idea is that we can show that crime is the outcome of intolerable constraints and if we improve these, crime rates should fall. We do not know if this is true, although we assert that we need not know much in order to approve of all such ameliorations. Yet we go further than that, by offering a criterion for amelioration even of constraints that may be quite tolerable. We observe that some reductions of crimes are outcomes of legislations that remove not constraints but temptations. And we wish to generalize this commonsense observation.

members of the two subcommunities to change places. (This is the abolition of ghettos.) This is not news, so the question is: Why do we not use this technique more often? The answer is more complex, but at least it explains why more educated societies employ softer means of law enforcement with better results than less educated societies, where laws are stiff and ineffective. It is not only that the law-abiding societies can afford less forceful measures; it is also that the gentler measures are so often far more effective. This is especially true regarding drug abuse because, clearly, it is already quite adverse in consequence without threatened legal penalties. Instead, all such vice has social roots that we should study and alter accordingly. Increasing the level of punitive measures (and its certain failure) may paradoxically bring about this improvement in public attitudes toward recreational narcotics.

To reiterate, the selfish conduct in prisoners'-dilemma situations is that of betrayal of partners, and legislation should help render such betrayal unpalatable. However, this is not always the case. When only a few individuals in a given society are involved in a prisoners'-dilemma situation, betrayal might be highly commendable and legislation should encourage it. The paradigm case here is whistle-blowing. Peers view the whistle-blower as a traitor; only the upholding of broader standards than those shared by peers help one to decide to blow the whistle. This, in turn, explains why so much stress on loyalty is prevalent in all criminal subcommunities. This is but one case of undesirable cooperation. A more sophisticated case is monopoly designed to curb competition among entrepreneurs. In that case, too, betrayal is right. Because joining a monopoly is obviously wrong, having joined it is no moral objection to betraying it. The rule is this: legislation should preclude those cases of prisoners'-dilemma situations where the partners are all members of a given society. Specifically, legislation should preclude theft and similar crimes, in which everybody can deviate to the detriment of the whole society. For, by our tentative hypothesis, legislation should render that conduct unpalatable that reduces public welfare. As long as the individuals involved compose only a small portion of society, constraining their options may benefit everyone else. These two examples, whistle-blowing and monopoly, are extreme cases so they are easy to handle. Other cases may be more complex and, hence, too problematic for us to consider. Sometimes they serve as material for semifictional stories of the crime world, which are popular because they avoid polarization and show that most of us are neither saints nor sinners. This is very commendable but only up to a point, the point being the blurring of the difference between those who are more on the side of the saints and those of the sinners. When popular taste finds ever greater appeal in such moral ambiguity, wise legislators should institute a study of the situation.

It is surprising how many norms that we generally recognize as sufficiently simple to be incontestably morally commendable are often easily explicable as cases in which the norm makes betrayal too unpalatable. One example is the public response to theft on the beach: it is seen as a disturbing betrayal of trust and invites violent response from passersby. The willingness of the London police to be unarmed is another example: when it works, it does so because London criminals have a negative attitude toward cop-killers: they consider them traitors.

These cases are unusual. Most other cases are regulated by the law. This, in turn, is explicable due to legislation aimed at making betrayal in prisoners'-dilemma situations too unpalatable. This is so, even though the analysis of such situations is new and legislators are still not familiar with it. To this more common category of reasonably efficient crime prevention through legislation belongs the popular hostility to many crimes, such as deceit, theft, and murder – and, at times, even wars between countries under normal situations. Moreover, the permissibility of many situations is likewise explicable as not being at the risk of creating prisoner's-dilemma situations too often, or at least not as a matter of course. Notice that by its very nature, a prisoners'-dilemma situation has to be fairly obvious to those whom it involves. Thus, when the public becomes aware of the prevalence of such situations, pressure on legislators mounts to render them less common or else the public ceases to view them as criminal. This holds for traffic violations and for drug abuse – and even to drug abuse while driving. This is a very difficult situation because it is hard to restore trust. This difficulty, needless to say, is the prisoner's-dilemma situation as initially described herein.

Liberalism as the Default Option

Legislation should suffice as a means to exclude most prisoners'-dilemma situations. This thesis is not the commonly received view

of the matter. We do not know if it is true, but we consider it the
default option, to deviate from it only when legislation fails. The more
popular thesis is that positive rules that increase human welfare are
superior to the mere removal of obstacles – that in addition to rules
that prevent conduct that obviously reduces human welfare, we also
need rules that encourage the increase of human welfare. This thesis
is usually asserted on general grounds, and supportive cases are not
hard to find. Thus, we know that it is not enough to claim, as Marxists do, that the abolition of private property suffices as a means to
increase human welfare. The rule that Marxists support is irrelevant
to the prisoners' dilemma, however, and we reject it without fear of
inconsistency. At least as the default option, we prefer negative legislation, leaving the positive to individual initiative. This comes close
to the views of classical liberal political philosophers and to the classical economists, including the neoclassical (i.e., Chicago) school of
economics – which is not limited to economics at all because it is
political – yet without the dogma that a free-market economy is the
best solution to all problems. That school has no criterion for legislation even though, like its predecessors, it demanded some legislation
to protect the freedom of the market. This has led to quite a few
problems. Consider this one: Is there a need for legislating truth in
advertising? The view of the neoclassical school was negative: the market, it said, would impose truthfulness on advertisers more efficiently
than the law, and it would require no additional law enforcement
agency and no bureaucracy to run it. But there is the need, it agreed,
to enforce contracts. Why does the neoclassical school of thought
demand laws against dishonest commitment but not against dishonest advertisement? It has no satisfactory answer to this question. We
have argued that we do need such laws on the supposition to make
betrayal too unpalatable to allow criminals to disrupt the system. An
example would be the need to prevent fly-by-night deception but not
deception by a trader who has invested a big sum in entry to the
local market. (This observation is commonsensical even though it
looks morally cowardly, thus dividing the local population between
the young and the experienced. It is in accord with trivial arguments
from games theory, which should make the young stop and rethink.)
The question, then, is: How effective is competition as a means for the
prevention of harmful advertising? Because viewing the situation as a

prisoners'-dilemma situation, we see that laws imposing truth in advertising may help maintain the effectiveness of competition. Our view thus rests on a hopefully testable tentative hypothesis. It helps differentiate between advertisements that require control and those that do not; if the differentiation is erroneous, then our tentative hypothesis can be modified.

To summarize, the dispute over the proper range of legislation required to maximize human welfare thus overlaps with the general dispute concerning liberalism. Advocates of classical liberalism go too far even by their own definition. Classical as well as neoclassical economists propose to limit legislation to the necessary protection of the market, but they have no criterion for this necessity and they cannot link it to the liberal demand (i.e., Spinoza, Hume, and Smith) that the law should render rational self-interest sufficient incentive for abiding by the law. Our tentative hypothesis leads us to prefer to limit legislation whenever possible and suggest that the aim of legislation should be to render unpalatable betrayal in prisoners'-dilemma situations. Non-liberals would add other rules. We prefer adding classical liberalism, but we consider it our default option: we propose additional rules that alter the interests of people who find themselves in a prisoners'-dilemma situation to make them less eager to betray their partners unless the betrayal is obviously in the public interest.

The prisoners' dilemma entered the literature in 1950 as part of game theory, as part of a search for counter-examples to the theory (of Adam Smith) that (in a free-market economy) private and public interests coincide, the theory that is the foundation of neoclassical ideology. Since then, the prisoner's dilemma has engaged not only game theorists but also psychologists, biologists, and later, also economists (who should first have renounced their unqualified faith in the neoclassical version of economic theory). This increased interest is due to a simple discovery: if two people play the game more than once, they tend to cooperate many times. Moreover, strategies for playing the game served software programs and enabled tournaments of games among programmers. The results were surprising. In one of the first tournaments, Anatol Rapoport's program won first place. His program obeyed the following strategy: start by choosing the cooperative option (i.e., do not betray) and then repeat your opponent's choice (i.e., betray in response to betrayal only). Later, a more sophisticated program won first place. Its strategy was to select in response to betrayal the cooperative option randomly in about one-third of the cases. A still different winning program was the recommendation to players to repeat their last move if and only if it was successful.

The winning programs were robustly cooperative, which is a hint at a very optimistic morality.[11] Does it suggest that rational selfish human beings should always select cooperative options? We do not think so. None of the winning programs was sufficiently cooperative; in this sense, they all disprove the idea that rational selfish considerations suffice for making us cooperative (not to say moral). Alas, private and public interests do not harmonize all by themselves; nor is sympathy sufficient as a regulator. Legislation is required to help make the market mechanism work. And, as all sorts of liberal political philosophers and neoclassical economists rightly keep reminding us, legislation can be messy and, at best, it is quite imperfect.

Utilitarian versus Kantian Ethics

The literature that centers on the analysis of prisoners'-dilemma situations comes to serve both the ethics of intentions, because its intent is to base the proscription of crime on selfish motives, and the ethics of consequences, because it explains the immorality of immoral conduct as criminal conduct and the criminality of criminal conduct by the inability of society to function without adopting general rules that proscribe them, which are usually taken to be punitive. Yet, the purpose of this prolonged discussion is also to examine the validity of the hybrid system of the two classical systems of ethics. We observe the frequency of the prisoners'-dilemma situations and those akin to it, the frequency of situations in which selfish conduct pays the cost of harm to the public interest at the cost of causing instability. This observation tests, and does refute, the idea that moral conduct is reducible to selfish rational conduct. Inasmuch as the classical moral theories, utilitarianism and Kantianism,[12] imply that ethics is rational, we find

---

[11] That this is surprising shows that the Spenserian misreading of Darwin is still extant despite Prince Peter Kropotkin's famous 1902 *Mutual Aid: A Factor of Evolution*.

[12] Immanuel Kant. fused moral and political demands quite incidentally, not to say thoughtlessly, escalating his demand that moral rules be universal to the inclusion of cosmopolitan politics. He made punishment rest on the assessment of law enforcement as necessary. This made anarchism problematic: if it is at all conceivable, then

here as much of a refutation of them as possible. But perhaps this is redundant: being that it is, indeed, common knowledge that all too often crime does pay and that, to a certain limit, society tolerates it and still functions well enough to be stable. This is why the young who are sensitive to justice hate the worship of stability that they find so common among their elders. So, we think our version of liberal philosophy is a possible tool for bridging the generation gap.[13] But we discuss the applicability of our views later.

It is amusing that philosophers should observe that sometimes crime does not pay and sometimes honesty is the best policy even in terms of selfishness. Yet we should observe this because the two traditional systems of ethics – the Kantian ethics of intentions and the utilitarian ethics of consequences – both declare the rules of ethics absolute.[14] (Remember, Kant forbade lying even in order to save a life![15] Jeremy Bentham was more commonsensical in his judgments, but not too much so.[16]) They are both at odds with the apparent truth from repeatable observation that the advantage due to trust or betrayal depends on their frequency. This already well-supported hypothesis,

---

Kant's justification of laws and law enforcement fails. (All demand for justification suffers from this kind of fault.)

[13] The first philosopher to have spoken against the view of social stability as a supreme *desideratum* was Karl Popper. Because stability depends on social and political controls, he observed, these come first, especially when democratically maintained. The classical view of controls, especially checks and balances, comes as ancillary. He viewed them as central conditions for democracy. It is now mainstream. Unfortunately, he declared himself Kantian, even though the mode of Kant's proof that any unacceptable act is immoral concerns stability, not survival. Thus, because he denounced lies as not universally admissible, he disallowed exceptions as threats to stability. Concern for survival instead of stability allows for them and renders ethics flexible and commonsensical.

[14] The rigidity of Kant's decrees makes them obsessive and seemingly very logical. There is no rule as to when an imperative is categorical or conditional. These terms belong to formal logic, but their use here with no criterion is not. Why is it better to forbid lies than to forbid them except to save a life? The categorical value of life shows Kant's view inconsistent or, at least, undetermined in principle.

[15] The austere, hyper-systematic character of Kant's writings makes them seem logical. His realization that compulsory education is illiberal and his determination to impose discipline on children made him declare them subhuman. (Do they become human as they leave school?) He said that their lack of discipline makes ethics inapplicable to them. This makes many adults subhuman too; this he did not notice.

[16] Bentham had a major contribution that is famous and that counts most both morally and politically. It is his demand that jails should be institutions for re-education. Yet, his *panopticon* is a design for a jail in which every prisoner is always watched.

obvious as it is, underwent tests by computer simulations (mentioned
at the end of the previous section). The tests agree with common
wisdom. The tests may be not sufficiently severe, and researchers may
seek more severe tests. For our part, we have no need for them because
we have no intention to advocate these ethical systems. Rather, we wish
to improve them.

Utilitarianism is the theory (of Hume) that individuals (1) do act
in their own self-interest as best they know how, (2) know best that
interest, and (3) are to be trusted best to take care of it. The last
component of this theory is not as psychological as it seems because it
belongs to liberal political theory. Moreover, one of the tacit assumptions of utilitarianism is the idea that competition benefits all on the
mere condition that participants conduct it in a civilized manner. This
tacit assumption is the core of the prevalent enthusiasm for the neoclassical (i.e., Chicago) economic theory. We argue that if and to the
extent that we all understand this tacit assumption in one and the same
way, and if and to the extent that this tacit assumption holds one way
or another to this or that extent, then it does deserve the enthusiasm it
evokes. Nevertheless, we say, even then, civilized conduct cannot hold
down the fort all by itself, so we have to try to extend the domain of its
applicability by wise liberal legislation and by the addition of whatever
is necessary for robust stability. This is a core message of the current
chapter; it is nothing new – Popper spelled it out in much detail,[17]
and staunch adherents to the neoclassical version of economic theory
admit it, no matter how reluctantly. Their debate with the Keynesians
is not about the need for government intervention but rather about
its best form – namely, the one that is the necessary minimum. The
former say that minimal monetary interventions should do; the latter
say that at times the intervention should be fiscal (i.e., government
spending money for some kind of public benefit when the market is
too sluggish) and generous (even to the point of wasting public funds
on projects that are a luxury). This issue is beyond the scope of the
present study especially because, in practical terms, new techniques of
intervention were invented (by members of both schools) that initially
neither party envisaged.[18]

[17] Popper, *The Open Society and Its Enemies*, Chap. 17, Sec. iii.
[18] The new practice of deficit financing to cover entitlements transcends the old debate.

Let us move, then, to the first two components of utilitarianism, the assumptions that individuals (1) act in their self-interest as best they know how, and (2) know best what their best self-interest is. That these assumptions are empirically amply refuted scarcely needs mention. Philosophers of the utilitarian persuasion, therefore, qualify their view when they are under pressure and say that it holds only for enlightened rational individuals. Even then they are in trouble because they do not mean to dismiss self-sacrifice as irrational.[19] Let us ignore this as exceptional. We may limit the utilitarian theory to normal cases, whatever these are; let us agree that individuals are enlightened and rational if and to the extent that they know (1) what their best interest is, and (2) what best advances it. Let us further agree that they (3) act on this knowledge as is best possible. With these qualifications, it is easy to endorse the utilitarian theory because in this version, the theory is vacuously true. (It still may be useful on the empirically testable assumption that small deviations from the conditions of the ideal lead to small deviations of its consequences. Alas, this too is hardly ever tested and, we suspect, because it is hardly ever the case.)

Alternatively, we may read utilitarianism as the recommendation to acquire knowledge and use it in selfish action. This renders the theory much more agreeable, yet we will not share it unless we find that it does not force the private and public interests to be in so much conflict as to threaten the smooth running of society. It is a consistently repeatable observation that our moral sentiment moves us to act unselfishly, especially in cases of such conflict. (Thus, although self-sacrifice is fairly rare, sacrifice is not.) Utilitarian philosophers repeatedly assert that people follow that sentiment because it is in their best self-interest to do so. These philosophers overlook the conflicts between the moral sentiment and selfish impulses proper. This too is not news: we know that selfish and generous people behave differently in difficult times. Advocates of utilitarianism hope that there will be enough generous people to counter-balance the misers. We do wish this to be true, but

---

[19] Hume mentions self-sacrifice at the end of his book on morals as a possible criticism of his utilitarianism. He explains it away by the claim that it purchases peace of mind. This begs the question because peace of mind is only attainable, if at all, by proper conduct, not by selfishness, no matter how enlightened.

we observe that it is not always true and that it seldom comes naturally, as the utilitarian philosophy supposes. Here, we see that the more advanced a society is, or the more civilized and well off it is, the more it fits utilitarianism – and vice versa. This, however, makes utilitarianism not too far from the truth only when limited to societies that have reached a high stage of civility and comfort. This raises the question: How should we bring any undeveloped society to this stage? This criticism is not new either. Kant voiced it when he spoke of bringing society to that state in the long and arduous process of "the education of humanity." In the meantime, he said, people have to behave morally even if it does not seem to them to be in their own best self-interest.

And so we move to Kantianism, where we hit a snag: If Kantian ethics is only needed because we are uneducated, then what is its status among the educated? The only answer that Kant's ethics permits is that, among the educated, the ethics of intentions and of consequences coincide. This is possible, of course, but only if all people possess the truth about every question that pertains to the conduct of their daily affairs. Kant's argument for this strong claim was that every morally acceptable rule is capable of presentation as a universal law. Why? We propose that the rationale for this is that a rule is acceptable if its adoption has a stabilizing effect on any egalitarian society, whereas its rejection will be destructive. Can self-interest not destroy society? Not if the conduct it leads to is confined to the civilized and those endowed with sympathy. For this, humanity has to be educated, Kant observed: he admitted that utilitarianism has an edge over his view because it is the better option for the educated. He said that the basis of morality is goodwill and declared that this sentiment leads to the categorical imperative, to the imperative that holds under all conditions. Whether this is so depends on what he saw as categorical. It is thus no accident that he was unclear about which rule is conditional and which is categorical: this difference much depends on wording, and the preferred wording should be the one that ensures that goodwill can serve as a sufficient basis for all morality in all societies. (Hence, to know how to word it, we should know what we want it to allow and to forbid. Therefore, the categorical imperative offers no guidance and is quite useless except as a justification for whatever we already want to justify. Alas, however, the preceding seems to most philosophers as no criticism at all.)

How does goodwill lead to the endorsement of the categorical imperative? Any answer to this question must be psychological, and the simplest psychological theory is that we sympathize with sufferings and we seek ways to reduce it – which involves thinking, of course. We have already suggested a minimal mode of thinking that seems to us to answer this wish. Here, let us discuss sympathy; we argue that this is enough and that it is better to ignore the rest of Kant's psychology. Because our view is psychological, we have to supplement it later with an ethics proper, but not with Kant's ethics, being as it is far too simplistic and much too vague.

Sympathy

People tend to sympathize with the sufferings of others. This is a psychological tendency that almost all of us share to a degree. We deem defective those who lack this tendency, viewing their defect as psychopathology or sociopathology, and we consider them immoral or, preferably, amoral – unable to possess moral sentiment or judgment.

People sympathize not just with human beings but with animals as well. This tendency explains animal moral rights, which prove that both Kantianism and utilitarianism are limited because they ignore animal rights. One might think that this criticism is shaky because animal rights are in dispute. Not so: torturing animals for pleasure is indisputably immoral. This case is extreme, but it suffices to show the limitation of traditional application of justificationism to ethics. It also points to two other items: (1) people deem greater sensitivity to others to be better but not when it incapacitates, and the debate about animal rights often turns on the question: How incapacitating is the practice of vegetarianism?; and (2) that there is no hope to settle the question about what kind and degree of sympathy are advisable.

The disposition to sympathize has evolved slowly over eons. Consider a conspicuous example: until recently, most people allowed for slavery as a matter of course; significantly, this is no longer the case. We explain this as a result of the growth of our ability to sympathize: in the past, slave owners did not consider slaves to be human "like us"; they kept in check their ability to sympathize with slaves.

The theory is popular that the abolition of slavery could not occur as long as it significantly served the economy. This theory is full of holes. In the West, slavery survived legally well into the nineteenth century; in Saudi Arabia, until the late twentieth century, and it is still not extinct there. As to aspirations for the abolition of slavery, efforts in this direction appeared in Antiquity.[20] Thus, sympathy has its own logic that is fairly independent of economic considerations. A more reasonable discussion should rest on a distinction between different forms of discrimination and exploitation and the recognition of the justice of anthropologists' claim that slavery comes in a variety of guises.

This leads to another practical suggestion: efforts to raise the level of sympathy by the proper use of the media can and do occur. The ability to understand moral thinking (in contradistinction to the ability to obey orders or satisfy expectations of others) grows with the ability to put oneself in other people's shoes – at an early age and throughout life.

Sympathy with others is varied. For example, in spectators' sports and at public performances of pop music, fans and groupies express not only sympathy but also identification. Sympathy to the sufferings of others is often expressed as the readiness to make sacrifices to reduce them: few people are willing to relinquish all their assets to one such end; the only ones who may do so view the making of a sacrifice as a way to tackle all ills. Again, to some extent, people show sympathy to the suffering of other animals, mainly mammals, which even manifests in the reluctance to kill roaches even while doing so.

Moral Disputes

To reiterate, we suggest the following psychological theories:

1. *The sympathy principle:* People tend to sympathize with the suffering of others and to consider immoral any act that increases it needlessly (Hume's principle).
2. *The welfare principle:* People are ready to consider which rules they would legislate if they were the rulers of the world aiming for maximizing human welfare.

---

[20] One of Popper's most resented assertions is that Plato testified to the existence of an Athenian movement against slavery that he greatly opposed. The Talmud indicates similar tendencies because it decrees that freeing a slave should not be done lightly (because all freedmen are converts and conversion is discouraged).

This theory relates to the following differences in moral intuitions:

1. Different parties have different intuitions in regard to sympathizing with the suffering of others.
2. Different parties have different views as to what means are best for increasing human welfare.
3. People's intuitions regarding sympathy may conflict with their own intuition regarding the means for increasing welfare.

As an example for the first case, consider disputes about the morality of abortion. Putting aside deliberate obfuscation, in many cases the difference in moral intuitions regarding abortion concerns religious dogma; however, sympathy for fetuses may also play a role: some sympathize with fetuses, viewing them as people, and others do not, viewing them as essentially no different from the brain-dead.

The dispute about the propriety of sexual freedom is an example for the second case, in which the moral intuition in its favor dismisses the view that sexual freedom threatens the survival of human society.

Finally, the dispute about the morality of globalization is an example for the third case. Like all reforms, globalization also has its victims, and many people sympathize with their suffering. This sympathy is expressed in moral intuitions that result in opposition to globalization. A different moral intuition yields support for globalization; it usually stems from the endorsement of the neoclassical economic theory that presents free trade as a promise of rapid benefit to all. But the globalization struggle may follow an ideological false dilemma, a contradiction amenable to more creative engineering.

These examples all lead to suggestions of the following ways to pursue moral disputes. A dispute that results from a disagreement about sympathy should lead the disputing parties to attempts to find arguments showing that the object of the contested sympathy does or does not resemble humans like themselves. For example, when discussing the morality of abortion, they may try to find how similar fetuses and humans are; indeed, this is what they sometimes do.

A dispute that results from a disagreement about a theory concerning human welfare should bring the involved parties to attempts to test that theory scientifically. For example, they can test the theory that free sex risks human survival or even find that it is already empirically refuted. It can be rescued from this refutation, of course, and this might be beneficial too: its advocates should seek scenarios in which different kinds of sexual codes are beneficial or detrimental to society or individuals. The same goes for propaganda for uncontroversial cases such as those of child abuse and child pornography, in which the scenarios are mostly one-sided. To be effective, all scenarios should be specific, detailed, and honest.

Finally, a dispute that results from the use of competing intuitions – for example, one based on the sympathy principle and the other on a theory concerning human welfare – should lead the disputing parties to attempts to present their intuitions to others in a comprehensive manner in the hope to reach some agreement and compromise.

More Against Reductionism in Ethics

The chief reason for the irreducibility of ethics to psychology or sociology is that, at most, a reduced ethics will explain the sense of duty, not duty itself. For example, A. J. Ayer said (*Language, Truth and Logic*, 1936) that the commandment not to steal is the expression of the revulsion against theft. This is a dual assumption: first, our sense of duty is an emotional reaction akin to some aesthetic responses; and second, there is no ethics (or aesthetics) independent of some individuals' feelings. We do not discuss the psychology of Ayer's assertion because it is marginal to his discussion. Rather, we should discuss his reductionism, his assertion that there is no ethics as such, no duty apart from a sense of duty, and so forth. If this is so, then those who suffer from kleptomania are exempt from any moral duty regarding theft. This is false. Ayer might respond that the victim of kleptomania suffers from ambivalence. So we can take as an example the case of the psychopath or sociopath who suffers no inner conflict. We assume that ethics applies to them too. To follow Ayer's argument, we should admit that our demands from the psychopath are on a footing with the psychopath's own indifference to morality. We normally think otherwise.

Note that our psychological theory in ethics presents a sufficient rather than a necessary condition for the endorsement of ethical judgments. There are duties that our psychological (and sociological) explanation does not cover, especially the duty to take care of ourselves. In part, it is well known that this duty is reducible to the responsibility to others – namely, not to be a public nuisance. Yet, we think it is also a duty to oneself to be kind to oneself. Tradition overlooks this duty on the (false) psychological supposition that most people are too selfish, they take care of themselves to excess, so that we need not encourage their bad trait by discussing the duty to take care of oneself. Quite a few errors hide behind this supposition, but the most relevant here is that the abuse of a duty leaves it a duty all the same. Suppressing consideration of it renders our ethics lopsided. Moreover, there are individuals, no matter how rare, who suffer from the disposition to torment themselves to excess (i.e., self-flagellism). They do deserve to learn that their conduct is immoral, especially because they are all too often encouraged in behaving cruelly toward themselves. Of course, self-flagellism is partly reducible to duties to others because it usually goes with some type of immoral conduct (e.g., xenophobia, self-righteousness). It is a general psychological observation that kindness to oneself goes well with kindness to others. Yet, we suggest that kindness to oneself is coupled with a sense of gratitude for our life and that this is morally commendable on its own.

Another no less important duty that is not discussed here and is neither reducible to psychology nor discussed sufficiently by psychologists is the duty to be critically minded. We do not elaborate on this; suffice it to say that we preach the autonomy of the individual as a supreme value, and that covers the duty to be responsible and thus the duty to be critically minded.

5

Politics

The previous chapter was devoted to discussions of applications of skepticism to moral philosophy. In this chapter, applications of skepticism to political philosophy are discussed. Once again, our starting point is that skepticism is true. We consider the implications of this to the questions that traditionally inhabit the agenda of political philosophy.

The Justification of Sovereignty

The basic question of traditional political philosophy is: What justifies sovereignty? Let us explain.

Rulers maintain their power even if some citizens oppose them, and then they rule by the application of force; the application of force is morally problematic. At the very least, it raises grave questions: Is this use of force moral? If so, under what conditions and on what grounds?

The most popular theory in the modern West is contractarianism, the doctrine of the social contract: rulers have the right to apply force because they are entitled to do it because they have the consent of their subjects to do so. This doctrine is obviously false because none of us has given blanket permission to the rulers to apply force, not even to apply force within the law, because none of us have given blanket consent to the law. Contractarianism came to distinguish between just and unjust governments, and it does not do that because no government is utterly just or unjust. Had it declared any government just, it would thereby declare it a utopia. Nevertheless, the doctrine is immensely convincing because we all prefer life in civilized society over life in the wild, all shortcomings of present society, its government, and its laws notwithstanding. Why then do political theorists insist on blanket permission? Because they want to justify government as such – that is, the rulers' use of force in general – without bothering themselves about the need to find separate justification or objection regarding any specific law; so much so that they triumphantly ask the anti-contractarians how they justify government.

This question implies the rejection of skepticism, of course. Because skeptics reject all (blanket) justifications, they reject all (blanket) justifications of all government. Then, it seems, logic forces skeptics to endorse anarchism, and the general view is that, obviously, anarchism is impossible (although many people have endorsed it; in 1930s Spain, it was a popular political party). Opposition to skepticism is often presented as a corollary to the opposition to anarchism.

Skeptics can meet this objection similar to the way they meet the objections to skepticism in epistemology and ethics: skepticism is the view that no statement is justified, neither the statement, "sovereignty is good," nor the opposite statement, "sovereignty is evil." Skeptics claim that anarchism is as unjustifiable as any other system of sovereignty and, therefore, skepticism does not imply anarchism, does not recommend anarchism, and does not necessarily even sympathize with anarchism of any stripe. Nevertheless, skeptics are at liberty to assume at their own risk that anarchism is right – or at least to sympathize with it – and some of them do. Disagreement as to what regime is preferable is more widespread than anti-skepticism, although only skepticism is consistent by admitting the reasonable view that some prolonged disagreements are reasonable, although it is logically impossible that all parties are in the right.

Not all political philosophers partake in this dispute, however. Some of them follow Popper and prefer to shift from the search for the most beneficial to the least harmful regime. We share this preference and, with Popper, we consider democracy as the least harmful regime – on the grounds that it admits its own imperfection in the skeptical mood and that it allows for criticism and for resultant corrections. We return to this point shortly.

Assuming that some kinds of sovereignty are better than anarchy, political philosophers turn to normative questions such as the following:

1. What is the best method of government?
2. What is the best method for the state to enforce its edicts?
3. What is the best method for the administration of social justice?

Allegedly, skepticism implies that the answer to all these questions is that sovereignty should be minimal. Because no one is immune to error, rulers' decisions might be erroneous; therefore, rulers should minimize their decisions, leaving the governments to function simply as the night watchmen and no more.

Not so, say the skeptics. Because these questions rest on the supposition that some normative political principles are justifiable, which the skeptics deny, their skepticism implies no answer to these questions and especially no positive ideology whatsoever.

But, if no normative political principle is justifiable, as skeptics claim, then another objection appears. Political disputes abound and demand their resolution one way or another in order to run practical affairs, and some resolutions are better – more rational – than others. Hence, politics is the search for these resolutions. Skepticism, however, denies that some resolutions are preferable and thus it blocks their rational resolutions. The skeptical answer to this is the same as its answer to the parallel objections in epistemology and in ethics: they seek rational resolutions too, but they are aware that these are limited because no judgment is utterly due to free choice, let alone rational choice. Our judgments are determined largely by psychological factors. This raises the question: What are these psychological factors and how significant are they?

Toward a Psychological Theory of the Morality of Politics

Under what conditions, then, does one endorse a given political judgment? As mentioned in the previous chapter, evolutionist anthropologists try to explain normative values by considering their contribution to the survival of the societies that adopt them. Thus, when they study political judgments, they seek Darwinian models that explain how norms are reinforced by natural selection – namely, models that present these norms as having survived due to their contribution to the survival of their practitioners and so also to that of the whole species.

We suspect that this view is naïve because survival is, at times, the result of a given characteristic and often despite it. In any case, our interest here is in a different aspect of the matter. The theory that we are looking for should explain neither the origins of normative judgments nor their contributions to survival; it should describe the psychological process that is responsible for current normative judgments such as they are and hopefully be testable, tested, and improved on. We are now in the middle of a discussion of moral–political disagreements because, traditionally, they are presumed less amenable to rational treatment than they really are. We also briefly discuss ontological political disputes, mainly about the economy, because democracies generally agree about the method for settling them.

Under what conditions, then, do given political judgments meet with general agreement? Let us emphasize here that we are discussing endorsement, not validity: we do not aim at the reduction of values to ontology – psychological, political, or otherwise. We suggest, then, the following tentative psychological theory, which contains a few assumptions. The first refers to moral, not political, values. This is not meant to reduce political theory to ethics or psychology. We come to the psychology of politics in our second and third assumptions that concern people's moral attitude to political change. Later, these should serve as a bridge to political philosophy proper.

Here, then, is our tentative theory:

1. People normally tend to sympathize with the suffering of others and to consider immoral any act that increases suffering (Hume's principle).
2. People are normally ready to consider which rules they would legislate if they were rulers of the state aiming at the maximization of the welfare of its citizens.
3. People are normally afraid that changes in the current methods of government would result in social and political disorders (or, at least, significant deterioration) and that these changes would bring about needless suffering.

The first two assumptions were discussed in the previous chapter on ethics. This is hardly surprising: we want politics to be moral and, to that end, we want political philosophy to rest on ethical foundations, shaky as they might be.

The (psychological) tendency to sympathize with the sufferings of others is almost universal, so much so that we consider those who lack it to be psychopaths or sociopaths – that is, amoral due to some abnormal deficiency. The implication for politics is that we may take it as the consensus that people object to any rule that needlessly increases suffering because they consider it immoral.[1]

As mentioned in the previous chapter, we note that people sympathize not just with fellow humans but also with other animals. This disposition explains the current campaign for animal rights. The very existence or even possibility of existence of these rights refutes contractarianism (i.e., the theory that justifies sovereignty by reference to a social contract) because it leaves no room for the discussion of the extent of animal rights, which seems eminently rationally permissible. Again, that animals do have some rights is not under dispute because torturing them for pleasure is indisputably immoral and some laws rightly forbid it.

According to the tentative psychological theory presented here, people are willing to consider which rules they would legislate if they were rulers of the state aiming at maximizing the welfare of its citizens. In what follows, we discuss the patterns of such rules.

Contractarians claim that utilitarianism is refuted by the following thought-experiment. It is easy to imagine a case in which hurting one (possibly innocent) person raises the total welfare of others, although this conduct is obviously immoral. (Thus, for example, as Jorge Luis Borges noted in his "Three Versions of Judas," it has never occurred to anyone to defend the crucifixion as moral on the grounds that it

---

[1] This hypothesis is politically extremely weak because even the Nazis declared the suffering they inflicted necessary; although they declared their alleged inferiors only subhuman, they declared that killing them was necessary. The Nazi philosopher, Martin Heidegger, also refused to condemn this conduct on the grounds that it was a necessary act of war. Whatever we say of such excuses, the very need to make the excuses for this conduct displays agreement with hypothesis that rejects this conduct. What is surprising is not our hypotheses but their sufficiency. Hence, the weaker they are, the better.

brought salvation.) This thought-experiment refutes the identification of moral conduct as causing an increase in general welfare. This refutation does not apply to our tentative theory: the statement that people prefer to maximize welfare is only part of our tentative theory. Because it also asserts that people sympathize with sufferers, and considering the victim of our thought-experiment, they will judge immoral the conduct that it describes.

Another objection to our tentative theory is the claim that human rights and citizens' rights are not only means for raising welfare but also expression of some noble principles. We agree and see no criticism here: we view these principles as means for raising welfare, but we have no intent to declare that this is the exclusive characteristic of these rights. We suggest that this should do for passing judgment on legislation. It is best to judge proposed legislation favorably or not depending on judgments of empirical hypotheses about the best way for legislation to raise welfare. Otherwise, legislation gets entangled in needless disputes on principle that would only delay urgent reforms. For legislative ends, it should suffice to propose that an item is considered favorably on (hypothetical) reasons: under present conditions, implementation increases respect for human welfare most. Rights are useful as a type of shortcut because usually we cannot calculate the expected influence of actions on the welfare of all citizens. Moreover, because proposed laws on rights also depend on what is no more than tentative empirical hypotheses, we should better consider them tentative, try to test them before implementing them, and treat their implementation as further experimental tests of the hypotheses that support them. We suggest that this enhances the respect for the principles of human rights and citizens' rights because it amounts to the willingness to withdraw a proposal if it turns out to cause suffering – hopefully out of respect for these very principles.

This leads to a practical implication: in disputes about questions pertaining to the enactments of new laws concerning rights, opponents may try to refute claims that they would raise welfare most. Moreover, all legislation should be automatically open for reconsideration, perhaps even after an agreed-on test period. Perhaps it is advisable to constitutionally institute a temporary enactment of every bill before it is fully enacted and a separate authority for the purpose of supervising the tests of new laws beforehand.

The Fear of Social Disorders

The fear of social disorders is normal because it is common: most people fear that social disorder will unexpectedly bring all sorts of suffering in its wake. Therefore, they fear great changes of the systems of government because, for all they know, these changes may lead to social disorder and thus to needless suffering. This may be explained by the application of the economic or quasi-economic idea known as the law of diminishing marginal utility. No one denies that, typically, small financial differences mean more to the poor than to the rich. Now, because changes of the system of government might fail (and we learn from history that this is regrettably too often the case), this law makes it sensible to initiate a change in any system of government only if the expected gains are considerably higher than the possible losses or if the injustice it is expected to rectify is considerably greater than the injustice it will unwittingly engender. In this sense, under normal conditions, as Popper observed, some degree of conservatism may be rational and even the default option – to be upset only in cases of urgency, of great social distress or risk, of significant opportunity, and of expectations that the new legislation would bring about great progress fairly quickly.

This explains why the seventeenth-century thinkers who inaugurated modern political philosophy repeatedly endorsed powerful monarchism, even though today many consider it immoral. Indeed, even the English public, for example, supports British constitutional monarchy but would admit that, if they lived in a republic, they would not advocate powerful monarchy – which is the point of this discussion. The scarcity within politics of the endorsement of new and bold changes in norms is due to a scarcely avoidable ignorance coupled with a fine consideration for the possibility that reform might worsen rather than improve people's lot. So, the practical question is this: What changes in the current system of government are urgently required and/or greatly beneficial to upset this reasonable reluctance to endorse new proposals for reform?

Note that we are ignoring the dispute between radicals, reformists, conservatives, and reactionaries. As long as the spokespeople for these philosophies claim that certain political positions are more justified than others, as skeptics we object to them all, repeating our claim that no position is ever justifiable. When we interpret these positions as prescriptions for efficiently raising welfare, however, we object to them all because it is obviously better to judge matters case by case on their specific merits or demerits. This is particularly important when technological innovations are in the offing because one cannot tell what kind of technology will be readily available in the near future. It may be the case, therefore, that one position is more efficient at one time, whereas another is more efficient at other times. At most, we consider the choice between these philosophies as the choice of default positions. As such, however, our preference is for moderate reformism because it is liberal and fallibilist – thus, the default preference for increased sets of options for choice. Evidently, this liberal preference at times tends toward radicalism, at other times toward conservative politics, and at still other times toward neither. As for the reactionaries, we never want to share attitudes with them because their position seems to us immoral: misanthropic and pessimistic.

Political Disputes

To reiterate, we suggest the following tentative psychological theory:

1. *The sympathy principle*: People normally tend to sympathize with the suffering of others and to consider immoral any act that increases suffering needlessly (Hume's principle).
2. *The welfare principle*: People are normally ready to consider which rules they would legislate it they were rulers of the state aiming for the purpose of maximizing the welfare of its citizens.
3. *The conservative principle*: People are normally afraid of suffering from social disorders resulting from changing the current method of government, and this fear is at times quite reasonable.

In light of this tentative psychological theory, we find the following possible conditions for disputes regarding politics that rest on differences in intuition. Some disputes rest on the difference of intuitions in regard to sympathy for the sufferings of others. As an example, we presented in the previous chapter the dispute over the morality of abortion. Other disputes result from different views as to what best increases human welfare. The disputes between advocates of free enterprise and socialism are also straightforward examples. Still other moral disputes are explicable as disputes wherein the intuition of one party is the outcome of considerations that rest on sympathy, whereas that of the other is the outcome of considerations that rest on the welfare principle because, in some given cases, different intuitions may initiate conflicting political proposals. The dispute about the morality of globalization, mentioned in the previous chapter, is the most topical example. Consider European farmers: abolishing subsidies for them will ruin their lifestyle, and we sympathize with the suffering that this move incurs. Yet, according to the neoclassical economic theory, free trade is beneficial for all concerned within a relatively short time span. This should obviously hold for all Europeans, farmers and non-farmers alike. The farmers' negative response, then, may be rooted in their ignorance of economic theory or in their having sufficient familiarity with it to harbor distrust or else in their readiness to pay a high price for the preservation of their lifestyle. But perhaps the farmers have a vague, general fear that the promised future compensation for their immediate loss may not arrive for any reason whatsoever. This last item is a different matter altogether, one that renders conservative attitudes generally rational. Indeed, most historical moral disputes are explicable as the result of different parties having different expectations regarding risks due to changes in the system of government. Again, disputes about the morality of monarchism are an example of this case.

The preceding discussion suggests ways for pursuing moral disputes in politics. A dispute rooted in a difference of sympathies should lead the disputing parties to seek arguments showing similarity or dissimilarity between the object of the contested sympathy and humans like them.

A dispute rooted in a disagreement about a theory concerning welfare should lead the disputing parties to attempts to test the theory scientifically. For example, they can test the theory that socialism or systems that practice relatively free enterprise, or any other system, is more conducive to welfare increase. At times, these tests amount to the implementation of different systems in different countries in an effort of the less successful to learn as much as possible from the more successful. What exactly this amounts to is open to further dispute. Here, we see that the pluralist political philosophy that is so popular today gains its greatest support and the best rationale from healthy, commonsensical skepticism of the kind that we share.

A dispute that rests on competing intuitions – for example, one based on the sympathy principle and the other on a theory concerning welfare – should lead the disputing parties to attempts to discuss their intuition with each other in the hope of reaching some agreement or compromise.

Finally, a dispute that rests on a disagreement about the risk implied by changing the system of government can at times be resolved by testing the change on small scales and then gradually increase their size and reach the national scale. We consider one such example in the next section, but first let us admit that this very proposal rests on a value judgment: in modern society, we expect ontological disagreements to be open to empirical resolution and demand that they should be resolved, and we expect that other ontological disagreements should be tolerated as much as possible without causing disruption. Of course, the question of how much disagreement is possible without disrupting society is predictive from prior observation, thereby likewise ontological. It is possible to destroy society over an empirically irresolvable ontological disagreement. History is full of cases of this kind. Because all of the preceding has gained public recognition and approval, it invites no further discussion here. Let us conclude, then, by observing that commonsensical skepticism is conducive to tolerance – for good or ill.

The Dissolution of the Nation-State

We now indicate the way for the application of our tentative theory to another practical political discussion. The subject under discussion is the proposal to dissolve the nation-state in a series of rather rapid, simple moves. Early in the twentieth century, Russell and Einstein recommended the establishment of a world government, of one state for the entire globe. The European Union is going in this direction, but obviously not in as extreme a fashion as Russell had hoped.

Following our tentative theory, considerations of this suggestion raise three questions that should be placed high on the European political agenda for public discussion.

First, does this suggestion harm other people with whom we sympathize? This question is empirical. Many people have strong feelings about their nationality, and they emphatically declare that reducing the role that nations play in world politics will hurt them. This may be true but, in this case, many viable options are easily available for harmless compensations for the nationalists; the experience of the European Union may indicate some of them. And, wherever options are open, the matter is open to empirical investigation – both as to the change of the role that nations may play as an outcome of any proposed reform and to its impact on their individual members. And, we suggest, the investigation should proceed along lines indicated previously. The chief disaster to avoid in this case is war, especially civil war: because the chief aim of the exercise was to reduce the danger of war, it should be obvious that a wise move toward a world government is one that significantly reduces this danger.

Second, does this suggestion raise welfare? This question is also empirical. If a change that reduces the role of nations is implemented with any measure of success, especially by the reduction of the risk of wars and civil wars, then this in itself should raise welfare considerably. But, that very implementation, no matter how commonsensical it appears, may also disrupt the cultural life of nations, thereby alienating their members and thus being detrimental to their welfare. Moreover, it may cause social disorder in some states, thus reducing significantly the efficient management of its affairs.

Third, does the very transition to one world state cause social disorder? Obviously, such a transition is very risky; indeed, Russell's and Einstein's proposal for the establishment of a world government was considered more utopian than practical. The example of the European Union offers a practical gradual development toward this utopia, thereby minimizing the risk of suffering from disruption, social disorder, and even the decline of local ethnic culture. How far the European Union can expand without raising a new type of trouble is obviously not given to scientific prediction because no extant economic theory explains its success – not even the classical or neoclassical theory – and because the European Union introduced new measures of economic state intervention. Hence, the sane proposal is to remain on guard.

Democracy versus Dictatorship

Thus far, we have discussed the implication of skepticism to the moral questions within political philosophy. We now turn to the second implication of skepticism to politics – the implication of skepticism for the choice of the best system of government. We concentrate on the central choice, that between democracy and dictatorship, because these systems seem to be the only current practicable options. And, to render dictatorship palatable, we should immediately state that we have in mind dictatorship as benevolent and as well disposed as possible toward modernization.

Every ruler, a dictator or a leader of a most democratic state, must decide for people who do not participate in the process of making decisions about issues that concern them. This raises two questions.

Because rulers may look after their own interests rather than those of their citizens, the first question is: In which system are the rulers more likely to best pursue the welfare of the citizens? This question is value-laden, of course, because rulers may prefer to serve utterly different ideals. So, not surprisingly, the comparison between democracy and dictatorship is not currently under debate: the rulers in democracy are more likely to pursue the welfare of their citizens for fear of not being reelected (Spinoza). This, however, is observed only in democracies; political commentators often extrapolate it to other countries because they assume that it would also be observed there if they were democracies.

Dictators repeatedly declare this question begging. Their countries are not democratic, they explain, because they lack the necessary conditions. They further suggest that their population cares more for their traditional ways of life than for their own welfare (i.e., they believe them to be best for the attainment of higher standards of welfare). Hence, their dictators conclude, becoming democratic without further ado would only worsen the situation. Accordingly, when certain new general elections lead to the rise of fanatical fundamentalist parties, dictators may block a fundamentalist takeover by simply refusing to step down. Should they step down?

These dictators are not fools. They are right to observe that traditionalism is strong among their people; they are likewise right to observe that their traditional leaders are undemocratic and their tradition is at loggerheads with democracy. Now, the plain truth is that traditional people want both tradition and some fruits of modernity: weapons, material comforts, or both. No one has succeeded in combining the traditional ways of life of the less fortunate countries with the wealth that modern technology offers. (No matter how rich these countries may be in natural resources, their populations are poor – and what their natural resources purchase most often is modern weaponry.) So, the question is: How can populations of such countries develop sufficiently reasonable public debates about what the people want? Dictators who often say that they prepare their people for democracy and express willingness to step down when the time is ripe do all they can to prevent public political debates. What is to be done about this?

We do not know. In fairness, we assume that the dictators we depict are benevolent and wish to improve the welfare of their citizens, but we observe that they do all they can to impede public political debates, thereby impeding democratization. Should we let them be or force them to open public political debates? If so, how? Even these questions are intractably difficult.

There is an additional aspect to consider. Benevolent dictators who try to maximize the welfare of their citizens may still make a mess of things, thereby worsening their citizens' welfare. But this holds for democratically elected leaders as well. So, the next question is: Which system, democracy or (benevolent) dictatorship, is less likely to do harm?

Historically, rulers often claimed that they had access to divine knowledge (directly or via priests under their command) and that, therefore, they knew best what was good for their people. Here, we assume the skeptical view, according to which no system is immune to error so that access to divine knowledge, *per impossibile*, offers no more guarantee of the avoidance of all error than any other source of knowledge – not to mention the possibility that the Divinity may have other considerations than the welfare of this or that nation. (Indeed, few doubt the recent assertion that the Divinity was not too kind to the Chosen People.) No matter what the system of government is, implementation of its opinions may harm the population at large.

This is no counsel of despair. Psychology and the history of ideas can help. In particular, we contend, we know of no better way to help our neighbors to democratize than by improving our own democracy. As mentioned in Chapter 2, we may try to combat one of the biggest obstacles to democracy that is one of the interesting phenomena in the history of ideas, and it is this: most people do not like to admit error, and rulers are no exception. Like other humans, if not more so, rulers hate to admit that the positions they had publicly espoused were erroneous. They hate even more to admit that their opponents had previously voiced valid criticism of their opinions.

This psychological phenomenon grants democracy a second advantage over dictatorship. Like a dictator, a democratic ruler cannot be trusted to admit having erred. However, contrary to dictators who stay in power and perpetuate their errors despite criticism and disaster, democracy can hopefully replace its elected government by peaceful means – by refusing to reelect them or otherwise deposing or impeaching them.

Many politicians try to avoid being refuted by espousing irrefutable slogans. For example, instead of suggesting detailed plans for decreasing poverty, they may claim no more than that they consider it a bad thing or that they will apply social policies against poverty that they describe much too vaguely for them to be open to critical assessment. This leads to a practical suggestion mentioned in Chapter 2: when politicians present their positions and plans, we – the citizens – should insist on hearing refutable versions of them; we should prefer candidates with refutable ideas. This way, we may improve the rationality of our choice in elections. Incidentally, this is a matter of general education of the citizenry. So, there is a point to the excuse of dictators who say their people are not yet ready for democracy. Yet, these dictators do their very best to prevent their people from achieving proper education – particularly democratic education – in favor of defunct traditional education. And, of course, the best way to acquire democratic education is to establish democracy, however imperfect it may be, to the extent that it is at all workable and somewhat more. This does not solve the problem for a country that is not ready for even a poor democracy. For that, what is needed is a government that is willing to provide for basic education and widening the circle of people involved in the decision processes of their government. Here is the place, perhaps, to mention the plan of Habib Borgiba, the erstwhile president of Tunis, to ship thousands of young adult citizens of a non-democratic poor country to rich democratic countries for a few years of education.

6

Aesthetics

Skepticism in Aesthetics

In previous chapters, we discussed epistemology, ethics, and politics. In this chapter, we discuss another field in which skepticism is applicable: aesthetics. We left it to the last because there are fewer objections to skepticism in aesthetics than elsewhere, due to a combination of two factors: (1) nihilism being regrettably a respected contender in aesthetics, and (2) the confusion of nihilism with skepticism that is the root of the prevalent hostility to skepticism. Perhaps there is also less dogmatism about beauty than about other matters, possibly because, regrettably, thinkers do not take beauty sufficiently seriously. It is serious all the same. It influences our lives. People make great investments in it – in the arts and in personal grooming. We argue about paintings to hang in the museum or in the home and what kind of building to construct and which cosmetics fit which person best. In what follows, we offer a new fragmentary and tentative theory of the judgment of beauty. We suggest that this fragment is applicable to discussions about beauty in order to increase its rationality and reduce its unpleasant emotional aspect.

Traditional aesthetics comprises the traditional studies of the following question: What kinds of aesthetic judgments are valid – that is, certain or at least plausible? This question arises because people argue about aesthetics, and such arguments imply that there are aesthetical criteria, explicit or not, and that they are open to discussion. Hence, then, beauty is not just in the eye of the beholder.

Although in full agreement that beauty is not just in the eye of the beholder, we endorse the skeptical response to the traditional aesthetic question: no aesthetic judgment is certain or plausible. There is no aesthetic knowledge; no aesthetic judgment can be ultimately justified: all aesthetic judgments are tentative. When they rest on existing criteria, these criteria themselves are tentative and hopefully open to improvement. (We can reject our criteria when they perceptibly lead us astray.)

Aesthetic discussions regarding the rational basis of aesthetic knowledge are quite analogous to those in epistemology, ethics, and politics. The idea is popular that skepticism in all of these fields yields as corollaries some absurd statements. In aesthetics, these statements are still analogous to the traditional objections to skepticism elsewhere, but slightly less so, in that they are slightly less prevalent in aesthetics than elsewhere.

The arguments against skepticism in aesthetics rest on the view that it yields the following absurd consequences:

1. There are no aesthetic rules; aesthetic nihilism is true.
2. Rational settlement of aesthetic disagreements is impossible.
3. The aesthetic judgments of art critics, museum curators, architects, and so forth are not superior to the aesthetic judgments of the aesthetically ignorant.

Let us consider these assertions and show that they are not corollaries of skepticism, thereby diffusing the traditional objections thereto.

The first of these objections to aesthetic skepticism is the claim that it implies nihilism. This objection rests on the following false claim: if no aesthetic judgment is certain or plausible, then no aesthetic judgment is true or right. This is a confusion of truth and certainty (or plausibility). It leads to the denial of the existence of doubtful truths. Contrary thereto, skepticism includes the following claims:

1. No aesthetical judgment is certain or plausible.

Nevertheless,

2. Some aesthetic judgments are right, correct, happy, and so on.

To see that a doubtful aesthetic judgment can be right, consider genuine aesthetic disagreement among serious, reasonable, fairly knowledgeable individuals, like those that occur regularly among curators or art critics. Such disagreements easily turn up whenever a new fashion appears. They are often rational. In such cases, each of the conflicting possible judgments is reasonable and doubtful; still, as the dissenting parties reject each other's view, at most only one of them is right.

The second of these traditional objections to aesthetic skepticism rests on the view that it blocks all rational resolution of aesthetic disagreements. The skeptical answer to this is the same as its answer to the parallel objection in epistemology, ethics, and politics: the objection rests on the assumption that aesthetic judgments are due to choice alone, but they are not. Our aesthetic judgments are largely determined by psychological factors. This raises the question: What are these psychological factors? We address this question shortly.

The third of these traditional objections to skepticism is that it leads to the absurd conclusion that aesthetic judgments of art critics, museum curators, architects, and so forth are not superior to the aesthetic judgments of the ignorant. If no aesthetic judgment is certain or at least plausible, then there is no justification for these expert judgments and, therefore, they should not decide which painting should be hung in the museum or which buildings should be constructed.

This objection to aesthetic skepticism is analogous to the similar objection to epistemological skepticism. Both rest on the false assumption that rationality requires justification. In one sense, judgments of experts and nonexperts (in any field) are equal; they are all fallible. Nevertheless, the function of art critics, museum curators, and architects is explicable in terms of non-justificationism. Experts foresee or claim that they are able to foresee the taste that eventually will become popular. For example, art critics and museum curators judged that impressionist art was beautiful when most of their public disliked the impressionist style and so rejected their paintings with hardly any examination. The experts foresaw a popular shift in taste and they were vindicated: nowadays, most of the public judges these paintings exceptionally beautiful. This is not to ascribe to experts the power of prophets. Their forecasts may rest on reasonable ideas. First, they are more receptive to new ideas, usually by being more critically minded about old ideas. Second, they are able to see what the innovative artists are trying to do, which enables them to assess their success or failure. Note also that aesthetics is less vulnerable to classical rationalism because artists are seldom satisfied with their output to the extent that they cease to seek improvement. (In this way, aesthetics differs from science, in which the dissatisfaction may apply to the frontiers of knowledge even on the assumption that past scientific achievements are perfect: artists do not consider perfect even the greatest works of art.)

Aesthetics and Beauty

Until the eighteenth century, philosophical discussions of aesthetics employed the words *beauty, beautiful,* and their cognates. They were concerned with criteria for the beauty of beautiful objects (including beautiful people). Nowadays, they mostly avoid this kind of locution in preference for the word *aesthetic* (or *aesthetic quality* and the like). Presumably, the word *aesthetic* has a technical meaning. Although it was introduced in philosophical contexts and it was supposed to be rather technical, many popular discussions are devoted to arguments about the right definition of the aesthetic. This is surprising because, in such cases, a word means what the people who introduced it wanted it to mean. (And if we do not know what this meaning is, then we had better not use that word because words should be our servants, not our masters.)

The main problem with the concept of the aesthetic is that it blocks rational discussion. Because we do not have strong intuition regarding the proper use of the concept of the aesthetic, we cannot refer to such intuition to criticize any thesis about aesthetic qualities. We have no objection to the use of the term *aesthetic* as identical to the term *beauty*, and we often follow suit because the latter term is in general use and, generally, people have stronger intuition about what is and is not beautiful than about what is and is not aesthetic. Still, it is largely agreed that there is a difference between the beautiful and the aesthetic. Some natural scenes or events or people or animals and their performances (e.g., the elegant swift movement of a tiger) are beautiful even though they are scarcely works of art. Some art is great and moves us deeply but is not beautiful (and is not meant to be), and some art is renowned for its beauty but not judged aesthetically as very impressive. We recognize works of art that are not beautiful to have aesthetic value. The classical examples are the famous paintings by Hieronymus Bosch and Pieter Breughel the Elder. In modern times, this phenomenon is much more common; at least, protest art is a familiar sort of intentionally unbeautiful products that are generally deemed valuable, not only for their social or political messages (because not all of them are considered to have aesthetic value). We return to this point shortly.

Toward a Psychological Theory of Beauty

When discussing the second traditional objection to skepticism in aesthetics, we claimed that our aesthetical judgments are largely determined by psychological factors. This raises the question that we now consider: What are these psychological factors and how can they serve us? That is, for a given aesthetical judgment, under what conditions do we endorse or refrain from endorsing it? Under what conditions do we judge beautiful a certain (natural or artificial) object or performance? Finally, as usual with us, we want to find how these psychological factors help to enhance our ability to enjoy art and what, if anything, we can do about them.

Many philosophers discussed the meaning of the concept of beauty. Kant, for example, claimed that beauty is disinterested pleasure; that is, what we judge beautiful is what we enjoy while having no practical interest in it. Whether this is true has been subject to endless debate. The debate is not relevant to the present discussion about the psychological conditions conducive to that judgment because Kant did not suggest any.[1]

Evolutionary psychologists claim that our aesthetical preference is explicable as contributing to survival. They declare beauty to have been initially sexual attraction: attraction to beautiful members of the opposite sex, they say, is due to their being healthy and suitable for procreation. For example, a nonsymmetrical appearance is unattractive because it may be due to a deformity caused by sickness. Also, women

[1] Kant's concern with aesthetics is still unclear. He had no particular love for the arts. Possibly he wanted aesthetics to be as universal as ethics. But here, he could offer no criterion and therefore no transcendental proof: a society with no morality is impossible, but he could imagine a society with no art. Schiller criticized Kant's ethics: its separation of the practical and the moral renders it impossible to commend the decent treatment of friends. Applied to aesthetics, this is devastating: by Kant's view, the labors of amateur artists are more beautiful than those of professionals.

find muscular men attractive and beautiful (or handsome, to use sexist terminology) and this, of course, helps the survival of offspring in two ways (i.e., reproductively and protectively). Men may find women with flat bellies attractive because the opposite may indicate that they are pregnant. Yet, there is a limit to this: local tastes vary as to whether thin or fat women or fragile or sturdy women are the more attractive; so, obviously, such explanations are limited.[2] Nonetheless, they hold at most in relation to the beauty of humans and need not be relevant to other aesthetic judgments, such as those about beautiful landscapes or wild animals or paintings.

Ancient philosophers offered two principles of beauty: symmetry and harmony. But, it is obvious that not every symmetrical object is beautiful (e.g., a simple office building might be symmetrical and boring, even ugly), and not every beautiful object is symmetrical (most paintings are not).[3] The same applies to harmony. We do not quite know what is harmonious (the word is very inexact, in both its original Greek and contemporary usage). Not every object that we judge to be harmonious do we also judge beautiful (e.g., we often judge excessive harmony not beautiful, perhaps because we judge it maudlin or kitschy), and not every beautiful object is noted for its harmony unless the concept of harmony becomes so broad that it renders the thesis trivial. Several scholars have claimed that we judge an object beautiful when its proportions meet with the golden section[4] or another simple ratio. This cannot be true because the golden section and simple ratios are rare when applied with precision and ubiquitous otherwise because they can then be found in almost any piece of furniture – although it is obvious that not all of them are beautiful.

---

[2] The difficulty is met by the hypothesis that people seek spouses who look like their parents (perhaps in line with Freud's theory of infant sexuality). This hypothesis is amply refuted, so they claim that it is statistically corroborated. We have not verified this but we nevertheless suggest that the vagaries of criteria for the beauty of fashion models also disprove this hypothesis.

[3] The hypothesis about symmetrical paintings deserves study: some highly obsessive people paint only symmetrical pictures, especially female genitalia. And symmetrical inverted triangles do appear even in museums of modern art.

[4] The golden section holds between two segments if the ratio between the sum of those segments and the larger one is the same as the ratio between the larger one and the smaller.

We propose the following psychological fragmentary and tentative theory: what we judge beautiful has a form that (1) is unexpected, (2) is ordered (i.e., not chaotic or accidental), and (3) does not appear as the outcome of some ill-fated event.

Let us offer some examples. Noble metals are considered somewhat more beautiful than base ones; indeed, their colors are infrequent and, as such, rather unexpected. Polished bronze is appealing, too, although somewhat less so. Similarly, flowers that have unusual colors or shapes are considered more beautiful than common growth, unless their color or shape indicates damage or sickness. For example, very large flowers (e.g., lilacs) are rare and are considered beautiful. On the other hand, cold weather in the middle of the summer is unexpected but not judged as beautiful because it is explained as an accidental phenomenon.

Works of art are judged beautiful only on the tacit assumption that they are not easy to produce. In this sense, they are unexpected. For example, efforts to decry modern abstract paintings often appeared as good imitations of them drawn by accident, by children, and by monkeys in the zoo. The assumption that drawing reliable images is not easy causes the tendency to judge such drawings beautiful. So does the assumption that it is quite difficult to string into poems some suggestive words in rhythm and rhyme; it causes the tendency to judge such poems as beautiful. When George Bernard Shaw wanted to decry drama in blank verse, he tried to show how easily composed it is.[5] Similarly, photographs are deemed non-art because they are easy to produce. The answer to this criticism is that the items selected for exhibition are a very small portion of a set from which they were selected and just because of their rare virtue. Indeed, both writing and photography are easy to do but difficult to do well.

One may expect here similar criticism from the chaos theory: some fractals are beautiful. Now, most fractals are chaotic and not judged beautiful. The suggestion that all fractals are chaotic is mere semantics.

---

5 When Marcel Duchamp wanted to declare the art scene phony, he presented a common object as a work of art. For this, he chose a urinal, in order to stress his contempt. The object of his choice is no work of art: its rarity that has won it a place in a museum is that he is the one who chose it – and his choice was arbitrary. We return to this issue later.

Some are very simply ordered and are seen that way; such fractals are rare and may be beautiful.

As these examples suggest, when judging art, we consider some targets that the pieces of art should meet (e.g., good likeness, rhymes) and assume that meeting these targets is not too easy a task. This makes the works of art that meet them rather unexpected. However, it is beyond the scope of this book to discuss the question of how these targets are determined.

We discussed unexpectedness in Chapter 3, in which we claimed that people endorse new beliefs in order to reduce the unexpectedness of the world. Here, we add that people enjoy viewing unexpected phenomena as long as they are not the outcome of ill-fated events. When there is no risk, we enjoy the challenge of the unexpected for the alleviation of boredom. We return to this issue shortly.

The Evolution of Art

Art has its transient fashions. As Gombrich stated, the history of art is explicable as a process of problem solving. Consider the history of painting: much of it is explicable as a series of methods to present the three-dimensional world in which we live on two-dimensional walls, carpets, canvases, or paper. Each solution that was invented through the history of painting was intriguing; as such, each meets the condition of unexpectedness. However, after some time, the solution became familiar, and then its application became more expected, and then a new unexpected solution was sought, perhaps after the problem deepened. Then, to find new solutions, newer problems were sought, usually those akin to the older solutions. For example, at the beginning of the Renaissance, the use of the principles of perspectives was intriguing and considered to be art. But, when the theory of perspectives became familiar, drawing a picture according to the rules of perspectives turned out to be a rather technical mission, and thereby not sufficiently challenging, not art proper. A new problem then appeared and it had to do with lighting: How can light and shade help entrench the sense of perspective and render a painting real? Paintings with obvious sources of light were depicted, and the light and shaded parts followed the rules of optics. This led to diverse variations, such as a painting of the baby Christ as the source of light, or strongly colored parts of a painting that enhance its composition, or, alternatively, paintings of interiors with soft light. All this, however, does not explain how some artists used these techniques to create great masterpieces that stand far above the rest of their kind.

Non-Beautiful Art

Our fragmentary and tentative theory explains why we judge as artful some non-beautiful exhibits. Placing them in museums is unexpected and so meets our condition of unexpectedness. For example, a urinal is not expected to be in a museum. The urinal itself is not beautiful, but the action of placing it in a museum (as a creation of Duchamp) was unexpected, not accidental, and not the outcome of an ill-fated event; as such, it had an aesthetical value like that of beautiful exhibits. Of course, it was not much of a surprise and the little surprise value that it had soon wore off. Therefore, we call it a gimmick and do not ascribe to it much aesthetic value. This raises the question: When does getting used to an idea reduce its aesthetic value and when not? For one thing, because repeated experiences of a gimmick wear it out, we call it a gimmick and forget it. But this is not the whole answer; we return to this discussion later.

Beauty and Pleasure

Most aestheticians agree that seeing beautiful objects or people is pleasing. Why? The answer to this question is beyond the scope of this book. A viable hypothesis is that we enjoy reviewing interesting phenomena, and the interesting is unexpected. The pleasure of viewing the beautiful, therefore, is like the pleasure of reviewing interesting phenomena (but not the other way around). In both cases, we enjoy revealing the unexpected.

To see this, let us compare viewing the beautiful bodies of members of the opposite sex and understanding a beautiful theorem in mathematics or a scientific discovery. Viewing beautiful bodies is attractive and, indeed, when we call them attractive we usually mean it both sexually and aesthetically. Yet, from the aesthetic viewpoint, Rembrandt's painting of coarse Hendrickje is much superior to his earlier painting of his lovely wife, Saskia. This is an example of the divergence between sexual and aesthetic attraction, which agrees with our fragmentary and tentative theory but clashes violently with the evolutionist explanation of beauty. This is hardly avoidable because most adaptations outlast their original survival value with unexpected results.

There is a famous sinister aspect to the aesthetic experience and one that makes many individuals hate art. It is the demand that educators make of their charges. It is bad enough to demand that students learn their lessons; the additional demand that they like the lessons is much worse. The conflict between the dislike of compulsory art and the pleasure of its enjoyment is intolerable. At times, this is the result of our educational system; at times, however, it is the outcome of dogmatic adherence to some arcane aesthetic theory, such as the idea that beauty is linked to the golden section. It is difficult to know how close an accepted proportion should be to the magical number 1.666, and it is amazing how much conviction the Pythagorean theory of small proportion has, especially in music. A priori, it is impossible for the same theory to hold for both diatonic scales and their series of modifications up to the well-tempered scale and beyond. As aesthetics, this theory is pathetic; as psychology of aesthetics, it is naturalistic, so the very possibility of stylistic variation refutes it, and these variations abound.[6]

A way out of this refutation is to postulate that of every two variants, one is more beautiful than the other. But this postulate is preposterous. The fragmentary psychological theory advocated here, by contrast, makes it amply obvious that a change of style may be welcome even if it turns out to be of little lasting aesthetic value. Indeed, all artistic changes are such that their novelty assures success as long as it is not taken as chaotic, unlike its lasting aesthetic value: this is open to the successful inventiveness of the artists who use it. (The invented technique should be used in ways that keep it fresh.) This is why so often innovation meets with public hostility that turns into

---

[6] The presentation of the Pythagorean theory and the overtone theory as one and the same, despite the famous great variety of alternative scale systems from the diatonic to the well tempered, and noting the use of the trill, tremolo, and vibrato as deviations from either – not to mention the willful deviations from the right tone that piano tuners impose on instruments and that styles by which opera singers are recognized – all illustrate the tremendous conflict between the desire for variety and for uniformity.

public enthusiasm that then fades into indifference; indifference is the ultimate destination of most works of art on their way to oblivion.

Tragedy

Many aestheticians, from Aristotle to date, found surprising the enjoyment of watching tragedies: because tragedies are sad, why do people enjoy watching them? Aristotle suggested the catharsis theory: we enjoy not the sad story but the experience of having watched it; we like to watch tragedies in order to have our funds of emotions purified by having them exhausted. Freud suggested a similar theory.

Our fragmentary and tentative theory explains better and in a simpler manner the possibility of judging some tragedies as beautiful. We do not expect stories to excite us because we know that they are unreal, products of the imagination. Therefore, when we watch a tragedy that does excite us, it catches us by surprise,[7] it meets the condition of unexpectedness (as well as the other conditions), and, as a result, we enjoy it and then we may – and at times do – judge it to be beautiful. This raises again the question: How, then, do we enjoy repeatedly watching a tragedy? Why do some but not all tragedies – or any other type of art, for that matter – weather repetitions and even win increased appreciation? We now come to this discussion.

Repetitions (1)

On the face of it, our fragmentary and tentative theory is in plain conflict with the empirical observation that we enjoy the repeated experience of the same aesthetic event, whether reading a poem, watching a drama, or visiting the same museum to see the same masterpieces. Because in these repeating visits we are familiar with these aesthetic events, they are not unexpected. How, then, can we judge them beautiful?

Our answer to this objection is that the beautiful works of art are unexpected because they are rare achievements, and this kind of

---

[7] Groucho Marx reports in his autobiography how much harder it is for an actor to draw laughter when costumed as a clown than otherwise because the joke is then so expected: given that clowns should raise laughter, we challenge them by resisting their jokes, he explained.

unexpectedness does not change by repeated visits. A painting that displays an expressive face is unexpected relative to our expectations of what can be (easily) drawn, and this unexpectedness is not decreased by re-watching. Likewise, a drama that keeps us excited each time we watch it is unexpected relative to our expectations of being excited by an unreal story. The question about why a certain drama excited us is beyond the scope of this study. However, the fact that we are excited when re-watching a drama is not more surprising than the fact that we get excited by watching it the first time because we already know that the story is not real.

This is not the whole story, of course. Different people enjoy repetitions for different reasons. Some do so to avoid the challenge of novelty. Others find repetitions worthwhile in finding in it new layers overlooked at first, especially if the work in question is new and challenging. Also, the repetition may serve different roles. William Somerset Maugham, the famous English storyteller, reported that he usually read a good story at least twice, the first time to enjoy it and the second time to see how it was put together. Our own part of the discussion is trite by comparison: we observe that, if the repetition is boring, we tend to dismiss the work of art as minor. Thus, if one can sum up the surprise of the detective novel by the justly famous punchline "the butler did it," then reading it a second time is impossible (unless the first time is flatly forgotten). The most prestigious detective novel is Dostoevsky's justly famous *Crime and Punishment*, which begins by telling the reader all that there is to know about the crime. The challenge for the author that keeps the reader glued to the page is to show how the detective forces a confession out of the criminal. Moreover, the author's intent was to combat moral nihilism, and the challenge is in the question: How well did he manage to do that? Also, here is an intriguing and important question: Is the book's aesthetic value dependent on the moral aspect of its story? We choose to skip this item.

Repetitions (2)

On the face of it, our fragmentary and tentative theory is also in plain conflict with yet another empirical observation related to repetitions. Many pieces of art include repetitive elements. For example, strings of beads and decorations on carpets or buildings, as well as musical works, include repetitive components. Because these elements are repetitions, they are not unexpected; yet, some repetitive works are judged to be beautiful.

Our answer to this objection is that it is not the components that are unexpected but rather the patterns that they display. Indeed, repetition is the means by which a pattern is displayed, whether in a building, a symphony, a carpet, or a necklace. We observe these items in search of patterns in them, and we judge them to be beautiful as we observe some interesting, unexpected patterns. The simplest example is a mosaic: in many cases, it consists of identical stones, each colored with one or another of very few colors. But it is the picture that we see, not the stones. Another equally conspicuous but less common example is Escher's technique of etching. His works comprise simple elements whose repetitive appearance integrates in counter-expected ways, such as an optical illusion (e.g., water flowing upward). Optical illusions are somewhat surprising, and their use is often judged a mere gimmick. Escher repeatedly utilized gimmicks and always in his specific way: it is not any single appearance of an item but rather its repetition, the pattern as a whole, that gives the illusion, and he plays with it, showing his spectator how it evolves by laying bare its stages.[8] Thus, the illusion is his clever means for enhancing the pattern that his work displays. That he used the same idea in many of his works may lead viewers to tiredness. This phenomenon, however, is extraneous to art: tourists hungry for art may find the effect of visiting one cathedral after another tiring and flat. This is a famous phenomenon called the *déjà vu* effect. Those tourists then have to rest before they may continue to visit more cathedrals with renewed pleasure. Whether or not they are beautiful cathedrals, tiredness makes them all equal and therefore non-art, but only as long as it lasts. Art may outlast tiredness, and great art certainly does.

For another example, it is well known that in music, a sequence of tones that makes for a melody is not beautiful if it exhibits a pattern that is too expected (as in playing a hurdy-gurdy) and it is not beautiful if it does not exhibit a noticeable pattern (as in chaotic random

---

[8] Artists may use the banal, be it a gimmick or a hackneyed idea, as challenging. This happens in every art form.

sequence). It is clear that the sequence has parts that are unexpected but accepted all the same as "making sense" once noticed. We judge a melody beautiful when we discover a rather interesting (i.e., unexpected) order of notes. This is not to say that on repetition of listening to the same melody its freshness will remain; that depends on whether it keeps us interested or starts to bore us. To mention another familiar phenomenon, when a new style of music appears, we may find the patterns difficult to notice, and then we judge those works to be chaotic and therefore of no interest. When we then learn the new language or the new style and see patterns in works that follow it, we gain appreciation, and then we can judge the musical pieces as expected or unexpected, as the case may be.[9]

This also explains why it is that when a new style occurs, the market may quickly be flooded with imitations of successful works – namely, works in the same style or exhibiting similar patterns, Soon, the public learns to discriminate, and the flood of much work that we judged first as great art and then as not so great becomes a trickle of great art that we judge classic and bear repetition thereof. Again, the question about what repetition survives and what sinks into oblivion is not a matter for this study to adjudicate, except to say that what stays keeps attracting our attention and, thus, our interest. It may be trivial to say that good art is not boring. Yet, we suffer so much boredom under the guise of art that the idea that boredom and art are enemies still deserves repetition. Not for long, we hope.

Pretty Average Faces

Another seeming refutation of our fragmentary and tentative theory is the empirical observation that was discovered in the nineteenth century by Sir Francis Galton: people judge as beautiful the merged image of randomly collected faces (within one social context) into one by superposing and averaging them. These merged images of faces are meant to be average faces – they have averaged-size noses, averaged-size eyes, and so forth. Because the average is expected, it is contrary to our fragmentary and tentative theory demanding that

---

9 This view of style is greatly influenced by the work of Sir Ernst Gombrich, especially his *Art and Illusion*, as well as his *Norm and Form*.

beautiful faces should be unexpected. This criticism is just. It has an easy and convincing answer, though, as follows:

1. Psychological research has repeatedly indicated that, when watching faces, we attend to very small differences. Therefore, the range of size that we grasp as average is very narrow, so being within this range is infrequent.
2. An image consists of many visible parts. In an average face, every part is average. As previously mentioned, the probability of each part to be average is low. Hence, a face all the parts of which are average is very improbable, much unexpected.[10]

Psychological research indicates also that some beautiful faces are far from the average (again, locally speaking) – for example, a face with large eyes and lips and a small nose. Such faces meet our fragmentary and tentative theory in that they are (1) infrequent and so unexpected, and (2) not due to some ill fate.[11]

Humor

The learned literature deems humor to be a part of aesthetics. Two ideas have been suggested for explaining humor: the incongruity theory and the superiority theory. The incongruity theory is the suggestion that the perception of incongruity makes us laugh. For example, many jokes create expectations that are suddenly shown to be completely wrong (i.e., Kant, Schopenhauer). The superiority theory is the suggestion that the sudden realization of our superiority is what makes us laugh, and we feel superior to the object of our laughter. For example, we laugh at a person who slips on a banana peel (i.e., Hume, Bergson). These theories have met with much criticism. They

---

[10] Perception is very intricate. We first seek to perceive expected patterns – particularly symmetries – then expected deviations from them, and then unexpected deviations from them.

[11] Let us repeat: it is easier to notice that some faces are interesting than that they are beautiful. At times, we have to decide that they are not sick deformities. At times, they grow on you, just as certain melodies that may first seem ugly do. Also, Gombrich noted, we may enjoy inferior pieces of art for non-artistic reasons, and this is quite innocuous.

are even more open to criticism when we consider them aesthetic theories – that is, when we consider all enjoyable jokes beautiful and vice versa. Here, we are concerned with aesthetics, not with laughter, because our tentative theory is only fragmentary: we do not assume that all enjoyable jokes are beautiful, but we try to explain why we deem beautiful those that are enjoyable.

Therefore, being a fragmentary and tentative theory, our view of beauty can partly agree with each of these theories but not wholly so. We assume that the perception of *momentary* unexpectedness may make us laugh. We should add, though, that our fragmentary and tentative theory makes better sense of these two theories. Incongruity is unexpected, but when it is immediately resolved, we laugh. It requires both an incongruity (as surprise) and its resolution (as no chaos). Likewise, we view slipping on a banana peel as an unexpected event that raises tension resulting in sympathy, so that the superiority is only part of the humor: when we see that the person suffers no serious damage, the tension dissipates and we laugh. But had the incident ended in a tragedy, we might not have laughed. (This is in contrast to the superiority theory, of course.) Here is another and more artistic item: in a drama, we often experience curtailed laughter or observe an actor laugh heartily and then end up in heart-wrenching tears. Humor is shortlived; true art endures.[12]

Non-Reductionism and Non-Relativism

To reiterate, our view does not reduce aesthetics to psychology. The wish to do so rests on the thesis that the meaning of every aesthetical judgment can be fully expressed as a statement about a psychological disposition or event. However, as previously mentioned, we do not present here an analysis of the meaning of the aesthetical judgment. Rather, we endorse a fragmentary and tentative theory that answers the question: What are the conditions for ascribing beauty? It is obvious

---

[12] Laughter is often an expression of sheer embarrassment. This is particularly true of truths said in jest. More sophisticated is the laughter that accompanies the resolution of embarrassment, particularly when it expresses deep and heartfelt sympathy with the embarrassed. Again, sympathy lasts more than the relieved embarrassment.

that these conditions do not explain all aspects of the aesthetical experience; however, analyzing this experience is beyond the scope of this work.

Aesthetic judgments are seldom unanimous. We usually differ in aesthetic judgments. This observation is so common that it comes in a hackneyed expression: "beauty is in the eye of the beholder"; it has a name: relativism. A difference is not always a disagreement, and a disagreement is not always rational. Reasonable discussions about it make it so. Still, one may declare all discussions unreasonable unless they come to a unanimous conclusion, and one may declare them unreasonable under any conditions. One may then say that they express some feelings (usually exasperation; at times, hostility) and no more than that.

Even if as a result of a discussion one party changes its view (e.g., if one sees beauty where one previously saw none), relativists may and usually will declare it irrational and, possibly, a process of helping one improve one's taste (e.g., Susan Sontag). This is an error: relativists should speak of a change of taste, not of improvement: improvement belongs to a better aesthetic perception. To reduce this improvement to psychology, one has to speak of the psychology of tastes as better or worse; by relativism, this descriptive psychology is impermissible: relativists deny that there is anything objective, such as beauty, by which to set a psychological scale. Judgments are part of psychology only on the assumption that there is something to judge. The hackneyed slogan, "beauty is in the eye of the beholder," is the denial of the very possibility of any aesthetic judgment and also only peripherally of rational arguments on aesthetics.[13] Therefore, the relativists must view all tastes of one individual as one given *datum* and all change of taste as the outcome of a sort of browbeating or coaxing, even if it comes from some expert in art appreciation or an art lover. Indeed, relativists have

---

[13] This view of tastes as not debatable because they are given leads critics to notice the coercion or at least coaxing that unavoidably involves all influences. Yet, a theory that allows for influences of only one kind is not open to criticism until its advocates specify their view in more detail. It is one thing to say that all taste is due to influence and quite another to explain the relative advantage of the choice of this or that taste to take the cardinal place in their theory, perhaps as the initial taste that we all share before we are open to the diverse influences that allegedly cause the diversity of our tastes, perhaps as the outcome of the desire to fit in a given social setting regardless of past history, or perhaps as a combination of these two explanations.

to view all possible influences of experts in art appreciation and all possible influences of art lovers as a kind of brainwashing. We therefore deem the very occurrence of rational aesthetic disagreements as a refutation of relativism. We present the following examples.

Aesthetic Disputes

To reiterate, aesthetics matters: people care about which paintings should be hung in a museum or in the home and what kind of building should be constructed. So they argue about them. In many cases, these arguments are emotional so they can easily become intimidating and even humiliating. Which ways, if any, are there to make these arguments friendlier? We suggest that the rationality of arguments renders them less intimidating and friendlier. How, then, can we make them more rational?

Our answer rests on the repeated observation that rational debates about art occur regularly. The fragmentary and tentative theory of beauty that we propose is that, to some extent, beauty is explicable as (1) unexpected, (2) ordered, and (3) not ill-fated. When arguing about a piece of art, we can try to explain its beauty to some extent by describing the way in which it exhibits these qualities. Following are two examples.

Consider disputes about modern art. In many cases, it is well known that the difference in aesthetic intuition about modern art concerns the ability to perceive patterns. Some do see patterns in these works and others see in them nothing but chaos. Such differences can be resolved by describing the patterns or, alternatively, by showing them scant and unsatisfactory.

Other disputes result from the selection of different objects or events that are supposed to be unexpected. The dispute about postmodern art is an example of this. By intention, postmodern art has vulgar aspects, and those aspects, admittedly, are not too beautiful. However, following Robert Venturi, one can see in the Las Vegas Strip, which admittedly has ugly façades, a certain opulence, a certain new artistic freedom that fits the background of the services that Vegas offers. This aspect is unexpected and, as such, it just may have the aesthetical value that Venturi finds there.

Our view is in contrast with the unfortunately quite common view that questions of art are decided by the inhabitants of the somewhat mythical art world: art critics, museum curators, gallery owners, and all sorts of connoisseurs. It is obvious that this common view blocks rational debate and is responsible for the passion of dissenters and the humiliation of outsiders. The fragmentary and tentative theory of beauty that we propose is thus situated very nicely between two vulgar views: one that says there is no aesthetic judgment and the other that says it is in the possession of experts. These are two poles of one myth (Claude Lévi-Strauss–style), and we can do better without this myth because it is not as helpful as the idea that improvements of aesthetic judgments are possible, and that rational debates and experts may help, particularly when experts criticize our aesthetic ideas and point at our shortcomings to the benefit of us all.

7

Conclusion

The Next Step

Thus, our brief survey comes to its conclusion. This final chapter summarizes the main ideas of the previous chapters with an accent on practical implications and offers a few parting thoughts.

Throughout this work, we presented radical skepticism, according to which no statement (or judgment) is certain or plausible (in the epistemological sense of these terms). We claimed that, contrary to popular criticism, skepticism is common sense, implies no absurdities, and permits alternative tentative theories of reasonability to discuss it critically, much in accord with common sense.

Complete error avoidance is impossible. This is practically important because under the influence of empiricism, many people still try to avoid error at all cost and then they find themselves doing so by clinging as much as possible to known observation-reports. This may lead them to present as few ideas as they can, limiting themselves to irrefutable ideas. Such ideas do not reduce unexpectedness; as such, they are uninteresting. As skeptics, we claim that aiming at error avoidance at all cost is itself a serious error. (As a popular edict goes, those who close their door to risk also close it to opportunity.) Sadly, we have to repeat the obvious: we do not recommend the conscious advocacy of falsehoods.[1] Rather, we recommend replacing the aim of error avoidance at all cost with efforts to meet these targets: (1) seek and

---

[1] Plato claimed that the Sophists were not serious because they defended conflicting views. Because of necessity this includes defense of falsehoods, it seems clear that they consciously defended falsehoods. Of course, they did not: at times, they defended conflicting views for not knowing which of them was true and in the search for the truth; at times, they did so as an exhibition of their skepticism. Plato hated both their skepticism and their advocacy of democracy.

present interesting ideas (i.e., ideas that reduce the experience of the unexpected); (2) avoid already corrected errors; and (3) try to find errors in current ideas, especially those that you yourself entertain. This proposal is, of course, an echo of Popper's.

Many of the arguments against skepticism rest on the ancient idea that skepticism imposes inaction. The skeptics – by these arguments – cannot justify their choice of beliefs or moral and aesthetical judgments, so they cannot justify any action and are limited to the choice between no action and senseless action. On the contrary, skepticism encourages the examination of many ideas regarding their truth or moral or aesthetic value, and the tentative judgment of many of them – favorably or not, as the case may be. Our beliefs and judgments are determined by psychological processes and rational discussions. Without trying to reduce epistemology, ethics, or aesthetics to psychology, we presented tentative partial theories about these processes. These tentative partial theories have wide-ranging practical applications. They may help resolve disagreements (not all of them, Heaven forbid) and they may help construct machines or processes that emulate human conduct.

Psychology

Our approach is more sociological than psychological; yet, in this work, we attended more to psychology. Western philosophy is magnificent because it advocates independence. Unfortunately, but quite understandably, this advocacy led it to an exaggerated concern with individual choices of opinions and attitudes about the avoidance of any submission to local prejudices in utter disregard for it and in an effort to avoid all error. Many philosophers recommend utter independence of spirit as a necessary means for these choices. Therefore, and still understandably, modern philosophy begins with the assumption that individuals are in full control of their choice of what to believe in, including their choice of a society to live in and even of a society to create. This is extreme individualism. It is glorious. Its application to research turned out to be the suggestion that the most basic human science is psychology, that all other human sciences are psychological at heart. For example, Hume and Smith, the fathers of modern economics, assumed that economics is a part of psychology and that it rests on the psychological assumptions about people's tastes that govern what they purchase and about their wish to be as well off as possible. This wish, they said, is to have a maximal purchase for a minimal cost. As it happens, the up-to-date view of the social sciences is that psychologism is a poor suggestion. The more recent philosophers tend to begin with society, not with individuals. This may easily lead to collectivism and, unfortunately, collectivism is usually anti-individualist and therefore is also anti-democratic. How should we avoid psychologism without falling into this pitfall of collectivism? This is a tough question.

One of the most dramatic aspects of philosophy is epistemology, or the theory of knowledge. Traditionally, under the influence of individualist morality, philosophers studied individual knowledge first. In the middle of the twentieth century, with the decline of psychologism, philosophy moved to public knowledge. This has left open the question: How does an individual member of a public take a share in this public knowledge? This question can be asked on many levels, including research, education, social stratification, communication, and more. In this study, we take the shift away from psychologism as given. This shift did not demand the betrayal of individualism and democracy, which is commonplace. What we add is that it does not demand the betrayal of psychology. This we have ventured to argue throughout this work: our accent is on psychology – and even with a vengeance – particularly because we take the public aspect more seriously than traditional philosophy does. The practical aspect of the linkage between the individual and the public seems to us to demand attention to psychology. We do not assume that individuals are as free as traditional philosophy leads one to assume. Rather, we seek to expand it, because we embrace the precious little liberty that we have and we want to show that learning its limitations may help improve thereupon. Surely, this suits well a study like ours that puts great emphasis on the practical aspect of philosophy.

The Meaning of Life

Much of the current literature of the popular philosophical schools that we have tried to ignore until now is devoted to the question: What is the meaning of life? The question may mislead because, literally speaking, meaning is linguistic: only words and sentences have meaning, and their meaning relates to what they convey. Taking seriously the analogy between language and life may lead to a view of life as meaningful only if it supposedly conveys something. But this assumption is obviously unserious. Still, we may suggest that one should have a purpose in one's life, which is often referred to as the meaning of one's life. This faces a similar difficulty: the suggestion that one should have one central target in one's life is quite strange.

We suggest the following. Plainly, we have various interests, including the interest in decreasing the suffering of others and reducing the unexpectedness of the world around us. Following skeptical considerations, however, we admit that we do not know what exactly our interests are, much less what the best ways to achieve them are. But we can study these questions and seek ever-improved answers thereto. This is the rational way to meet our interests. If one calls this suggestion the meaning of life, then we do not object. So, in some sense of the word, life does have meaning, and it is the one we try to give it.[2] Indeed, we experience this because if and when we lose it, we feel depressed. Hence, a healthy mode of life is purposeful and the examination of the purposes we have in the aim of improving them is the earliest and the latest concern of philosophy.

Some people say that they have ideas they cannot bring themselves to doubt. But, over any lifetime, it is surprising that some ideas come into doubt and others do not. Even the most general assumptions are subject to change. Take any field of inquiry with which you are familiar and ask yourself if you can share the certainty of your predecessors of a century or two ago – and if not, why not.

Finally, let us observe that, because skepticism is moderate, it is neither conservative nor radical; however, it is otherwise not able to adjudicate between the almost conservative and the almost radical. All we can say is that it allows for some moderate optimism, and we suggest that this is morally imperative (not as an assessment but rather

[2] The idea that life is meaningless is known as the thesis that life is absurd and is known as existentialism. The idea that existentialism is of supreme importance appears more frequently in the writings of Albert Camus than in those of its originator, Jean-Paul Sartre, even though Camus was the more life-affirming of the two. We find their concern defeatist: the question is not whether life has meaning but rather, as Popper stated it, if we dare give it any.

as a call for action). We may entertain a hypothesis that implies that doubt and change in belief can only amount to suffering. Such a hypothesis may itself be subject to doubt. This is a cause for hope. We may wish to forestall the danger of sheer credulity and to preserve the advantageous fruits of progress up until the present. We may use to that end caution and filter new hypotheses and information. This is also an entirely reasonable application of doubt. Moreover, there are countless repeatable observations of gain, improvement, and even positive emotion experienced in various processes of new belief formation possible only because of the ability to doubt. Hence, fear toward doubt in and of itself is irrational. Indeed, modern rational skepticism, the most successful outlook in all of history, remains honestly quite engendered of cautious optimism.

Glossary

ad hoc: the slightest modification of views under the pressure of criticism, meant to save them from criticism; changes made minimally and reluctantly

analysis: literally, dissection, taking apart; the opposite of *synthesis;* philosophical analysis is the spelling out of ideas in detail

autonomy (moral and/or intellectual): literally, self-rule; independence

collectivism: the theory that societies shape individuals and their aims; the theory that social ends precede individual aims; see *sociologism*

conservatism: the most widespread theory; it states that to fare well, society should follow and guard its own traditions

convention: social agreement, socially endorsed opinions and rules, arbitrariness

conventionalism: the demand that laws should be obeyed although they are conventional (i.e., enacted by some arbitrary agreement); the theory that science is binding only as a convention

criterion: a rule (or goal) for judging

critical attitude: the readiness and the wish to engage in criticism; see *criticism*

critical rationalism: the view that rational conduct involves trial and error, conjectures, and criticism

criticism: attempting refutation, to locate any error, fault-finding, even problem definition

deductivism: the view of science as based on axioms; intellectualism

empiricism: the theory that knowledge is wholly based on observations; the theory that only observations, if anything, justify theories

enlightenment: understanding; the theory that science will save humanity; *the Enlightenment:* an intellectual movement ruling the intellectuals in the seventeenth and eighteenth centuries

essence: the quality that makes a thing what it is; the opposite of accident, which is inessential

essential definition: the description of an essence; see *essence*

ethics: the rules of proper conduct; the theory of such rules; their justification

existentialism: the philosophy that says life is purposeless and that realizing this is the only salvation of the individual – it thus seemingly says nothing about society; in truth, as developed by Jean-Paul Sartre, it is a reactionary social philosophy thinly disguised as progressive and scarcely hides its contempt for common people

fallibilism: the view that no human endeavor is free of error

humanism: faith in humanity; the theory that all humans possess dignity to protect and enhance

individualism: the theory that only individuals (and not collectives or societies or institutions) are real; that only individuals have purposes; see *psychologism*

induction: the process by which scientific theories (allegedly) evolved from available scientific information rather than theory; the process by which scientific theories (allegedly) gain scientific justification from available information rather than theory

inductivism: the view of empirical science as resting inductively on information

intellectual frameworks: see *metaphysics*

intellectualism, a priorism: the theory that scientific knowledge rests on axioms the truth of which is attained by intuition; justification by intuition

logical positivism: the justification of *positivism* by the (absurd) claim that metaphysical utterances are inherently meaningless; the conceit that this claim follows from an existing, satisfactory theory of meaning; the conceit that this claim comprises a non-controversial demarcation between the utterances of science and metaphysics

Marxism: the theory (originated by Marx) that (the essence of) history is the history of class struggle; a school of thought that assumes a monopoly over radicalism and progressivism in order to cover up for its anti-democratic tendencies and contempt for common people

metaphysics: the first principles of physics; the metaphysics of any science is the foundations or the intellectual framework of that science

method: literally, way; scientific, metaphysical, or any other method is the (allegedly) proper way to do science, philosophy, or anything else

methodology: the theory of (proper) method; see *method*

nationalism: the theory that the proper citizenry of the state compose a (coherent) nation and the state is its instrument

nature: reality; the real; the opposite of appearances

paradigm: literally, chief example; a fancy and confusing name for intellectual framework; a fancy and confusing name for some given individual scientific theory that is a chief example of some given intellectual framework

phenomena: literally, appearances; experience

pluralism: the preference for a diversity over unanimity – of opinions, of denominations, of political ideologies, of scientific theories

positivism: literally, straightforwardly terse and to the point; the theory that philosophy has nothing to say or delve into; see *logical positivism*

proof: decisive justification; the act of making everyone see the truth of a proposition; showing that a proposition is unquestionably true

psychologism: a form of *reductionism*, the theory that, because only individuals really exist, all social science is actually psychology; the theory that backs individualism and was once progressive

Pyrrhonism: see *skepticism, traditional or Pyrrhonist*

radicalism: the demand to reject all tradition and all arbitrariness; the theory that unless one starts afresh utterly and thoroughly, all of one's effort is in vain

rational belief: (supposedly) scientific belief; (supposedly) belief based on proof or evidence; obligatory belief; incontestable belief

rational disagreement: disagreement in which it is not obvious which of the different sides is mistaken, in which the different sides have sound arguments for their own views and/or against opposite views

rationalism: the theory that one should use one's own brain to select one's lifestyle; classical rationalism is radical, modern rationalism need not be radical

rationality: the disposition to think and act rationally (i.e., critically); i.e., while arguing, presumably thereby justifying one's views and actions

reaction: literally, opposite action; backlash; the traditionalist (backlash) response to the radicals

realism: the theory that reality exists, that our experience emanates from objects, that there is something other than (behind) the appearances

reality: that which is behind the appearances, the solid behind the transient, the substance; see *substance*

reductionism: the idea that one science is really another – for example, the idea that psychology is really physics because we are computers of sorts; in the social sciences, there are two traditional versions of reductionism: the psychologism of the Enlightenment and the sociologism of the reaction; see *psychologism, sociologism*

reformism: the theory that the best practical approach (to society, politics, legislation, science – perhaps to all other matters) is (not to endorse and not to reject but) to try to improve it

relativism: the opposite of absolutism, the idea that the truth differs in different times and places or what the true ethic is; the denial of absolutism; although absolutists need not reject the relative, relativists are those who reject the absolute

religion (revealed and rational): doctrine plus ritual plus tradition plus the community of the faithful and its organizations

romanticism: the hankering for the past

skepticism: the view that proof is impossible

skepticism, traditional or Pyrrhonist: the demand to suspend judgment on every issue because proof is impossible, plus the view that the suspension of judgment brings peace of mind (*ataraxia*)

socialism: the idea that justice is impossible to reach unless (private) property is abolished; the proposal to abolish (private) property

sociologism: the theory that only societies (but not individuals) really exist and all social science is actually sociology; see *reductionism*

Socratic doubt: the readiness to examine every view, however obvious and/or well-established it may be

substance: the real; the utterly independent of everything else; the simplest and the unanalyzable; see *reality traditionalism:* the theory that the best way to run a society is to stick to tradition as much as possible in efforts to preserve them as best possible

ultimate values: the (presumed) axioms of an ethical system

utilitarianism: the idea that the highest good is the greatest happiness for the greatest number

Utopianism: the search for an ideal state

values: central norms or criteria by which to determine norms; whatever makes life worth living

Further Reading

Agassi, Joseph, *The Siblinghood of Humanity.*
Agassi, Joseph and Aaron Agassi, *The Continuing Revolution: A History of Physics From The Greeks to Einstein.*
Albert, Hans, *Treatise on Critical Reason.*
Asimov, Isaac, *I, Robot.*
Bacon, Francis, *Essays.*
Borges, Jorge Louis, *Labyrinths.*
Bronowski, Jacob, *Science and Human Values.*
Bunge, Mario, *Metascientific Queries.*
Descartes, René. *Meditations.*
Einstein, Albert, "Physics and reality", in his *Ideas and Opinions.*
Feyerabend, Paul, *Science without Foundations.*
Freud, Sigmund, *Civilization and Its Discontent.*
Gellner, Ernest, *Relativism and the Social Sciences.*
Gilson, Etienne, *Heloise and Abelard.*
Hart, H. L. A., *Law, Liberty and Morality.*
Heine, Heinrich, *Religion and Philosophy in Germany.*
Hume, David, *Essays, Moral, Political and Literary.*
Jarvie, Ian Charles, *The Revolution in Anthropology.*
Lakatos, Imre, *Proofs and Refutations.*
Malinowski, Bronislaw, *Magic, Science and Religion.*
Meidan, Abraham, *Skepticism is True.*
Oakeshott, Michael, *Rationalism in Politics.*
Plato, *The Apology of Socrates.*
Popper, Karl, *The Open Society and Its Enemies.*
Russell, Bertrand, *The Problems of Philosophy.*
Russell, Bertrand, *Mysticism and Logic.*
Russell, Bertrand, *Skeptical Essays.*
Schrödinger, Erwin, *Science and the Humanities.*
Wiener, Norbert, *God and Golem Inc.: A Comment on Certain Points where Cybernetics Impinges on Religion.*
Wisdom, John O, *Foundations of Inference in Natural Science.*
Wisdom, John O, *Philosophy and Psycho-Analysis.*

Bibliography

Hume, David. *A Treatise of Human Nature.* Edited by David Fate Norton and Mary J. Norton, Oxford University Press, 2000.

Montaigne, Michel de. *The Complete Essays.* Translated by Donald M. Frame, Stanford University Press, 1957.

Naess, Arne. *Skepticism.* Routledge and Kegan Paul, 1968.

Oakeshott, Michael. *The Politics of Faith and the Politics of Scepticism.* Edited by Timothy Fuller, Yale University Press, 1996.

Popkin, Richard H. *The History of Skepticism: From Savonarola to Bayle.* Revised edition, Oxford University Press, 2003.

Santayana, George. *Scepticism and Animal Faith.* First published 1923; reprinted by Kessinger, 2005.

Sinnott-Armstrong, W., and M. Timmons (eds.). *New Readings in Moral Epistemology,* Oxford University Press, 1996.

Index